A COLLECTION OF

PRAYERS *for* SCHOOLS

● ● ● ● ● ● ●

JAMIE PROUSE

Copyright © 2020 Jamie Prouse
First published in 2020

The right of Jamie Prouse to be identified as the author of this work has been asserted by him in accordance with the Copyright, Designs and Patents Act 1988.

ISBN: 978-1-910719-93-0

All rights reserved. No part of this publication may be reproduced or transmitted in any form or by any means, electronic or mechanical, including photocopy, recording or any information storage and retrieval system, without permission in writing from the publisher.

Published jointly by Jamie Prouse
and Verité CM Limited,
Worthing, West Sussex BN12 4BG
+44 (0) 1903 241975
www.veritecm.com

British Library Cataloguing in Publication Data

A catalogue record for this book is available from the British Library

Scripture quotations marked 'ESV' are taken from The Holy Bible, English Standard Version® copyright © 2001 by Crossway Bibles, a publishing ministry of Good News Publishers. ESV Text Edition: 2016. The ESV® text has been reproduced in cooperation with and by permission of Good News Publishers. All rights reserved.

Scripture quotations marked 'KJV' are taken from The Authorized (King James) Version. Rights in the Authorized Version in the United Kingdom are vested in the Crown. Reproduced by permission of the Crown's patentee, Cambridge University Press.

Scripture quotations marked 'NIV' are taken from the Holy Bible, New International Version (Anglicised). Copyright © 1979, 1984, 2011 Biblica. Used by permission of Hodder & Stoughton Ltd, an Hachette UK company. All rights reserved.

Scripture quotations marked 'NLT' are taken from the *Holy Bible*, New Living Translation, copyright © 1996, 2004, 2015 by Tyndale House Foundation. Used by permission of Tyndale House Publishers, Inc., Carol Stream, Illinois 60188, USA. All rights reserved.

Printed in England

*I dedicate this prayer book to my wife Charis
and my dear children— Bertie, Teddie and Lucie.
I love you with all of my heart.*

My deepest thanks to Chris Woodruff and Linda Howlett
for their incredible support, unwavering friendship and prayers.

Thank you to Canon J.John
for his encouragement and for his powerful Forward.

Thank you Louise Stenhouse,
who helped bring this together and gave much of her time.

Finally, to all those who gave me encouragement
to write and complete this book, I am blessed to have you in my life
(you know who you are), thank you!

'And let us consider how to stir up one another to love and good works,
not neglecting to meet together, as is the habit of some, but encouraging one
another, and all the more as you see the day drawing near.'

(Hebrews 10 vs 24-25 ESV)

'If my people, who are called by my name,
will humble themselves and pray
and seek my face and turn from their wicked ways,
then I will hear from heaven, and I will forgive
their sin and heal their land.'

(2 Chronicles 7 vs 14 NIV)

CONTENTS

A Note from the Author 1
Introduction 5
Collective Worship 11
Prayer Is 13
Foreword by Canon J.John 15
The Lord's Prayer 19

PRAYER TOPICS

A new year 21
Ability 22
Acceptance 23
Achievement 24
Action 25
Advent 26
Adventure 27
Advice 28
Ambition 29
Anger 30
Anxiety 31
Authority 32
Autumn 33
Awe 34
Beatitudes 35
Beauty 36

Beginnings	37
Being resilient	38
Being resourceful	39
Beliefs	40
Belonging	41
Bible	42
Body	43
Bravery	44
Bullying	45
Calm	46
Care	47
Celebration	48
Changes	49
Character/reputation	50
Charity	51
Choices	52
Christmas	53
Comfort	54
Commitment	55
Common sense	56
Communication	57
Community	58
Compassion	59
Compromise	60
Conduct	61
Confidence (in Jesus)	62

Conscience 63
Conservation 64
Consideration 65
Co-operation 66
Courage 67
Creation 68
Creativity 69
Darkness 70
Differences 71
Difficulties 72
Disappointment 73
Discovery 74
Dreams 75
Duty 76
Earth 77
Easter 78
Elderly 79
Empathy 80
End of school year 81
Endurance 82
Enemies 83
Enjoyment/fun 84
Environment 85
Epiphany 86
Example 87
Failing well 88

Faith	89
Faithfulness	90
Family	91
Fear	92
Floods/barriers	93
Focus	94
Forgiveness	95
Friends	96
Friendship	97
Generosity	98
Gentleness	99
Giving	100
Goodness	101
Grace	102
Guidance	103
Happiness/joy	104
Harvest/thanksgiving	105
Healing	106
Health	107
Holy people	108
Honour	109
Hope	110
Humility	111
Individuality	112
Influence	113
Inner-healing	114

Intelligence	115
Jesus, the first and the last!	116
Journeys	117
Joy	118
Justice	119
Kindness	120
Koinonia	121
Leadership	122
Learning	123
Leisure	124
Lent/Easter	125
Light	126
Light	127
Limits	128
Listening	129
Loss	130
Love	131
Loyalty	132
Manners	133
Me	134
Morning	135
Motivation	136
Moving On/Dreams	137
Music	138
New Term	139
Opportunities	140

Partnership	141
Patience	142
Peace	143
Peace (Inner)	144
Perseverance	145
Personality	146
Physical Health	147
Play	148
Pleasure	149
Prayer	150
Priorities	151
Protection	152
Punctuality	153
Readiness	154
Reciprocity	155
Recognition	156
Reflection	157
Reflectiveness	158
Rejoice	159
Relationships	160
Reliability	161
Remembrance	162
Renewal	163
Repair	164
Resourcefulness	165
Respect	166

Responsibilities	167
Reverence	168
Right and Wrong	169
Risk-Taking	170
Sacrifice	171
Safety (Community)	172
Safety (School)	173
Saints	174
School/Community	175
Self-Control	176
Self-Discipline	177
Self-Esteem	178
Service	179
Sharing	180
Silence	181
Skills	182
Spring	183
Stewardship	184
Stillness	185
Success	186
Summer	187
Sustainability	188
Talents	189
Thankfulness	190
Thanksgiving	191
Time	192

Tolerance	193
Treasure	194
Trust	195
Trust	196
Understanding	197
Union	198
Value	199
Winter	200
Wisdom	201
Wonder	202
Word of God	203
World Peace	204
World Suffering	205
Worship	206
Amen	207

A NOTE FROM THE AUTHOR

I have been a primary teacher for fourteen years and I currently work in an Anglican/Methodist foundation church school in Frome, Selwood Academy. I am married to Charis, we have three beautiful children (Bertie, Teddie and Lucie) and we currently live just outside of Bath, England.

Like many schools, weekly themes are used for acts of worship time, commonly known in schools as 'collective worship'. This book is a collection of prayers written over the past ten years, designed for use in any school setting by adults and children.

In 2009, I began to write weekly prayers based around a weekly theme: values, attributes, emotions, topics, celebrations, seasons and Christian festivals, among other things. I wrote a prayer to be used by all teaching staff (in class acts of worship), and/ or guest speakers and children (to be used in collective worship). During my teaching career, I have also encouraged children to write prayers too, which they do successfully when given the chance. Personally, writing prayers has been incredibly powerful for me, I hope the prayers in this book might bless whoever reads and hears them.

Since 1944, all state schools have been required to provide a daily act of worship that is 'wholly or mainly' Christian in character. I am aware that not every headteacher or teacher is a Christian, but collective worship/ acts of worship is still required by law and is often central to the ethos of many schools today. A prayer is required for an assembly to be called collective worship/ an act of worship – not many know this.

In the early days, I had observed that prayer was more than often the last thought at the end of collective worship or sometimes it was left out altogether. Prayer is important to me as a Christian, so I took on the role to change this and to promote prayer in my school. I include a biblical verse for each prayer, which I hope would be used **at the start of, or be the inspiration for** the collective worship/ classroom act of worship. To me, a bible verse is fundamental to every prayer- God's word, his advice, his guidance and his promises at the centre and the inspiration for each prayer, rather than my words.

Prayer itself opens a child's mind to something and someone greater – God. Collective worship encourages pupils to develop and reflect on their beliefs and helps to shape fundamental British and human values in the school community. It is my hope that this prayer book will help schools address some of these, by acting as a source of support, as a ready-made set of prayers for any school to use when and how and with whomever they choose. I hope children think deeply about each prayer and act on the message it delivers.

I have tried to ensure that the language of each prayer is purposefully simple (unlike those found in most prayer books), so that they are accessible to anyone, particularly children who they are designed for. The words encourage the development of spirituality in the minds of our young people and the hope is this: as our young people grow into adults, a message of kindness, love, tolerance, compassion and empathy (some of the key features of Christianity and many other religions) is encouraged and shared through such prayers. In my view, this will help to promote a more caring, thoughtful, outward-looking and considerate generation. As young people reflect and make up their own minds about the content in the prayers, the concepts and ideas discussed in them, I hope a fire for goodness and God begins to burn within them. I hope they begin to 'live the message' of hope, peace, joy, generosity, faithfulness, thankfulness and love.

This prayer book is not intended to replace any adult saying his or her own prayer during collective worship. A spontaneous prayer spoken from the heart is far more special, far more meaningful and personal than reading a prayer from a prayer book such as this. However, I hope this prayer book may help/give ideas or share the sentiments of the assembly theme in question, saving time and offering a helping hand to whoever chooses to use it. It may say exactly what you need it to, or it might encourage you to write your own. I hope this book can inspire assemblies and provoke deep spiritual thought.

A prayer that Jesus teaches us to pray, 'The Lord's Prayer', is the most important prayer of all. If we teach our children this prayer and help them learn this above any other, we will do our children and young people a great service. It contains adoration, thanks, apology, request for help and guidance, and puts God first. Above any other prayer in this book, it is the one prayer children should know by heart, even if they have no faith, hence why it is at the very front of the book, to show its importance above any other prayer written in here.

It is very important that no child should ever be forced to pray or say 'Amen'. Why should they and why would they, if they do not believe? However, if they are encouraged to respectfully listen to the words in silence as they are read, most will find it hard not to agree with the sentiments in the prayers. The values in the prayers are inclusive despite being purposely and unapologetically distinctive in their Christian focus. Children can be encouraged to write or say prayers too; in my experience, some of the prayers written by children are beautiful, raw, meaningful, powerful and from the heart.

I hope prayer becomes a focal point in school collective and classroom acts of worship again. I also hope that our children start to think about who we are praying to and why we might be saying such prayers, on such topics, values, celebrations and themes? As a child, I remember praying at school and thinking deeply about the words. They influenced my view of the world, how I thought about others and how I should behave. They made me a better person. Assemblies that started or ended with prayer gave me time to evaluate and reflect on the message I had received, and I hope that these prayers might do the same.

Finally and most importantly, I know from personal experience that prayer works, I would not waste time writing them if they did not. I hope this book of prayers for schools is a blessing to any school or educational setting that chooses to use it. I hope it is inspiring to anyone wanting to pray to God. And, I hope it is a help to those who don't know how to pray, offering ideas and support.

God bless,

Jamie Prouse

INTRODUCTION

Praying is primarily about talking to and then listening to none other than God. It is an incredible, mind-blowing opportunity to speak to our creator, our father, our friend, comforter and Lord.

In Genesis 4 vs 26, the first prayer is mentioned, the first indirect conversation with God since Adam and Eve walked with God in Eden. It says this: 'At that time people began to call on the name of the LORD' (NIV). **This is all that prayer is.**

Prayer does not have to be 'hands together and eyes closed'. This would stop many prayers taking place and is not what the Bible teaches. Prayer can happen with eyes open, whilst you walk, alone in a private, quiet space, in a church, or with friends – anytime, anywhere.

Praying can and should be done from any body position. The Bible mentions five:

1. Sitting (2 Samuel 7 vs 18)
2. Standing (Mark 11 vs 25)
3. Kneeling (Acts 7 vs 60)
4. Face to the ground (Matthew 26 vs 39)
5. Hands lifted up (1 Timothy 2 vs 8)

In the Bible, God commands us to pray: 'Then Jesus told his disciples a parable to show them that they should always pray and not give up' (Luke 18 vs 1 NIV).

And, Jesus himself prayed: 'Ask, seek and knock' as it says in the Bible (Luke 11 vs 9-13 NIV), so that we might **receive, find** and **walk** through the doors that God opens for us. God offers us something in exchange for praying, promises and reassurance he will answer them.

From the very beginning God intended his creation – humans – to talk with him, walk with him and obey him. When Adam and Eve disobeyed God in the Garden of Eden, humans stopped 'walking with God' and talking directly with him face to face. There was a relationship break-up because of human disobedience and sin.

From that point onwards, humanity now needed to **seek God** and **call on his name.** When we are in constant contact with God, we walk with him. Prayer allows us to be in regular contact with God and to remain in a good place where he comes first in our lives and we give him centrality above everything else – not an easy thing to do in the twenty-first century.

Love is best expressed for something or someone – humans were first created because God loves us all, thus giving humanity dignity and purpose. In designing us, he created us that we would have a relationship with him. The only way to do this is to live right, sing and pray – one could actually call this 'a life of prayer.'

With prayer, God answers. It is a two-way conversation. Usually the problem with this truth about prayer is that sometimes we are not listening; we are not in tune with hearing God's voice (which might be a whisper) and therefore we do not hear his response. So, we stop talking to him. This is our mistake. To resolve this, all we need to do is start speaking to God again (praying), or if we already do, pray more regularly- a stronger relationship will return once we begin to listen to God's voice and once we begin to see answers to prayers.

If prayer was simply humankind talking to a non-communicative God, who wouldn't or couldn't respond to thanks, requests, cries for help, what then would be the point? In the Bible there are over 450-recorded answers to prayer, proof enough that prayer works. Prayer is powerful; it is our access to God and finding out his heart for the world and for each one of us.

Lack of confidence, self-esteem and fear are some of humankind's biggest problems, as are jealousy, greed, want and selfishness. Praying against those things ('lead me from temptations and deliver me from evil') helps us to live well and purposefully.

In the Lord's Prayer (Luke 11 vs 1-4), Jesus provides five areas of focus for prayer:

> **1.** Honouring God's name – the focus on his everlasting glory ('Father, hallowed be your name').
>
> **2.** Asking for God's kingdom to come – the focus on his eternal will ('Your kingdom come').
>
> **3.** Asking for God's provision – the focus on our **present** ('Give us each day our daily bread').
>
> **4.** Asking for God's forgiveness – the focus on our **past** ('Forgive us our sins, for we also forgive everyone who sins against us').
>
> **5.** Recognising God's deliverance will be provided – the focus on our **future** ('Deliver us from evil').

The Lord's Prayer deals with our past, present and our future – it is an amazing prayer!!

Prayer is a way to help us do good, refrain from sin and have the most fulfilling and productive life we can, with God in control of our lives. Doing what God wants us to do restores our relationship with him. We find peace with God, with others and ourselves.

Sometimes, we are the prayer, or we can be the prayer! Instead of praying for a hungry person, we can give that hungry person food! The hungry person may have prayed for the very food you give to them. Someone who comes into your life to help you might be your answered prayer. God works in mysterious ways, all for the good of those who love him. We love him by being obedient.

When we pray coincidences happen. Pray about your greatest failures, then pray for the world. Be intentional in praying for family, friends, colleagues, neighbours and enemies. Why? Because when we pray things change. God responds. Praying also leads to caring! Getting into the habit of praying daily deepens our ability to care, love and change this world for the better. For children, this is invaluable learning and necessary to live their lives to the full.

Schools are made up of lots of people and God is concerned about what concerns us all. We all come from a different place, we have different experiences and we all believe different things. Praying for good things, God's guidance, thanking God for our blessings and asking for help, is incredible. It costs nothing, but it could be and it just could mean everything to someone.

Prayer in schools on values, on topics about anything, firstly puts the name of God back into the minds of his children; it offers an avenue for them to speak to him personally in reflection and shares what God is about. Prayers that speak God's words back to him are meaningful, powerful and faith building. They encourage nothing more than kindness, care, compassion, forgiveness and all the attributes he asks for in his people.

Here is my prayer today:

Father God,

May this prayer book be a blessing to anyone reading it, to any person listening to the words and hearing them in schools across the land. Bless our schools and all those who work in them, Father.

Jesus, may we learn from your teachings, your life and your parables about how to live. Help us to be more like you and place you first in our lives.

Holy Spirit, teach us your heart for the world and each one of us personally. Open our eyes to become better people. Prompt us to speak to you in prayer more often, trusting and believing, in faith, that you will respond to us.

I pray this prayer book brings glory to your name, Jesus.

Thank you, God.

Amen.

'The Holy Spirit produces this kind of fruit in our lives:

Faithfulness

Goodness

Kindness

Love

Joy

Patience

Peace.'

Galatians 5 vs 22 (NLT)

COLLECTIVE WORSHIP

An assembly is a group of people who meet together, usually to go through notices, important school information, etc. Unlike a purely secular assembly, collective worship should include religious views and expression. Pupils can be lead to an assembly but you can't make them worship, neither should you want to. Collective worship however, has always been about offering opportunity for spiritual development, teaching important human values and broadening young minds. Usually, acts of worship take place in a classroom/ spiritual room and collective worship in schools takes place in a larger space.

What collective worship does is provide a focus for personal development and reflection. It is an opportunity for our children and young people to reflect on the fundamental questions of life and to celebrate things of worth. The things that schools consider to be of worth (i.e. the school's values) are likely to be consistent with Christian and other religious values (e.g. honesty, compassion, trust, forgiveness, humility, courage, service, respect, justice, generosity) so it's not difficult to understand or see why school worship themes are 'broadly Christian' in character. Harvest, Christmas and Easter are also celebrated in most schools.

Religions provide lots of useful materials to extend pupil's thinking on these values. Schools are encouraged to develop a concept, theme, belief, or text for a week, or a term, exploring it from different faith and non-faith perspectives and what it means for each person, the school and society as a whole. Prayer should form part of the collective worship package; more frequently, however, a time of reflection takes its place when a prayer is not available or written by whoever is taking the collective worship.

'Pray in the Spirit on all occasions
with all kinds
of prayers and requests.'
Ephesians 6 vs 18 (NIV)

'For where two or three
are gathered together in my name,
there am I in the midst of them.'
Matthew 18 vs 20 (KJV)

PRAYER IS

- A devout petition to God.
- A spiritual communion with God, as in supplication, thanksgiving, adoration, or confession.
- The act or practice of praying to God.
- A formula or sequence of words used in or appointed for praying: the Lord's Prayer.
- Prayers, a religious observance, either public or private, consisting wholly or mainly of prayer.
- That which is prayed for.

Who are we praying to?
God the Father, Jesus (the Son) and the Holy Spirit.

What can we pray about?
There are different types of prayer:
- Prayers of praise and adoration.
- Petition – asking God for something.
- Prayers to say thank you.
- Prayers for others – intercession.
- Prayers of blessing.
- Anything on your heart that you personally want to talk to God about.

Where should we pray?

Prayer can and should happen anywhere. There are no set times to pray, it comes down to 'free will'. Pray alone, with others, in your home, out while you walk, in the car, while you prepare to sleep, literally anywhere!

When should we pray?

Prayer can and should happen at anytime of the day or night – God is always listening and is always ready to respond. Don't forget to listen to God, he will respond.

Why pray?

Prayer is simply talking or singing to God, depending on your mood and circumstances. Sometimes we feel compelled to pray out of need and desperation, other times we want to talk to God to thank him for a great day, or shout at him when we are down and need help, comfort and guidance. We pray because sometimes it is the only thing left to do and because we can. God asks us to pray, to ask him for things, for help, guidance and for comfort.

How do we pray?

The Lord's Prayer teaches us how to pray. When we close our eyes, or focus on God and just speak (even when we sing), this is prayer. It is not difficult, you don't have to be in a church or any other religious building, you can pray anywhere, anytime. Speak in your head until you feel confident enough to speak aloud to God.

FOREWORD

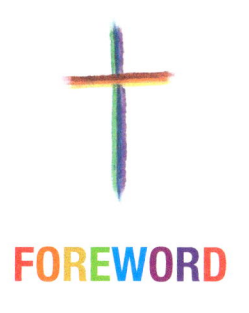

I'm delighted to write a foreword to this book of prayers for use in a school setting. In thinking about how we deal with children, not just in prayer but in everything to do with God and faith, I have decided that there are three important principles, which I am pleased to find in these prayers.

The first principle is that we must treat *children* seriously. We've all heard the dismissive phrase 'oh it's only for kids' and it's an unfortunate one. Children deserve the best we can offer. For one thing, they are valuable in their own right. In a culture in which children were not highly valued, Jesus treated them with a seriousness that surprised his own disciples (Matthew 19:13-15; Luke 18:15-17). Here, as elsewhere, it's an excellent idea to follow Jesus' example. For another thing, children are also important because – often faster than we are comfortable with – they grow up into adults. What we say to children about God can shape the way they think when they are grown-up. In fact, if we dig around in our own minds we can all surely unearth a variety of memories of how, as children, we were introduced to religion. Some of us have memories of words or actions that helped us think seriously about God and laid the foundations for a deep and valuable spiritual life. Sadly, others of us can recall a careless, clumsy or even callous treatment of God, faith or the Bible that encouraged us to drift away from God. Children need to be taken seriously.

The second principle is a mirror of the first: it is that we must treat *God* seriously. I suspect many people were 'put off God' at an

Prayers for Schools | 15

early age by teaching that presented him as little more than the proverbial 'old man on a cloud'. That careless trivialisation of the most serious of subjects has done a lot of harm. We need to do better in presenting the richness, breadth and depth of the Bible's teaching on who God is and who we are. The frustrating reality here is that the good news of the Bible is so clear and simple that a child can understand it. The 'big idea' at the heart of the Christian faith is that God so loved each of us that in Jesus he took our place and died for us so that we can receive forgiveness. That idea of 'substitution' is something that even the youngest can understand. Yet there is much more. There are riches in the Bible that should be taught to young lives: for example, the vital values of truth, love, forgiveness and hope. In talking to children, we need to treat God seriously.

The third principle is that we treat the *world* seriously. Childhood is a precious period that was always short but now seems to be getting shorter and during it we would all like to cocoon our children from the sorrow and suffering that there is in the world. Yet to seek to do this is a problem. In our modern age, even the youngest child cannot escape the knowledge that there are some seriously unpleasant things around. Where we cannot and should not protect our children, we need to present to them a wise and sensitive response; a response that models how we should react to such things. Children need carefully thought out material – like these prayers – that is appropriate and relevant for them. It is good and wise to aim to protect our children from our world's evils, but we must also try to prepare them to deal with what they cannot be protected from.

Let me end with a story that speaks volumes about the importance of what we teach children. There is a famous account of the great and vastly knowledgeable twentieth-century theologian Karl Barth being asked at a conference, when he was in his 80s, if he could summarise what he believed in a single sentence. The old man thought and simply replied, 'In the words of a song I learned at my mother's knee: "Jesus loves me, this I know, for the Bible tells me so."'

When you teach children, you teach for a lifetime. They need the best we can offer and I'm glad to see that these prayers do just that. When talking about God to children we all need to remember that teaching kids isn't kid's stuff.

J.John

Reverend Canon

www.canonjjohn.com

THE LORD'S PRAYER

Our Father who is in heaven,
holy be your name.
Your kingdom come,
your will be done,
on earth as it is in heaven.
Give us today our daily bread.
And forgive us our sins,
as we forgive those who sin against us.
Lead us not into temptation,
but deliver us from evil.
For yours is the kingdom,
the power and the glory.
Forever and ever.
Amen.

A NEW YEAR

Dear Lord,

We pray for the coming year ahead, this new beginning and all the opportunities that will arise in the coming year.

Bless our teachers and all the staff who work at the school. Help them to continue to work together to make this school a wonderful place to learn. We pray for every person, valued and vital to our community.

Help us as pupils to try our absolute best in all things, work hard and aim high. Help us to be caring towards each other and help us to follow the rules for the well-being of everyone.

Help us to shine this year and make our friends, our teachers, our families and carers proud of us!

Thank you for all we will achieve as a school together.

In Jesus' name.

Amen.

'For I know the plans I have for you, declares the LORD, plans for welfare and not for evil, to give you a future and a hope.'
(Jeremiah 29 vs 11 ESV)

ABILITY

Dear Lord,

Let not our abilities define us, but what we do with them.

Help us to channel our talents, gifts and abilities for good.

Teach us your ways, so that through good works we might praise your name.

Thank you that it's not ability that defines us, Lord, it is availability – to help, listen, support, befriend, care and love.

Amen.

'Now to him who is able to do immeasurably more than all we ask or imagine, according to his power that is at work within us, to him be glory in the church and in Christ Jesus throughout all generations, forever and ever! Amen.'

(Ephesians 3 vs 20-21 NIV)

'For as in one body we have many members, and the members do not all have the same function, so we, though many, are one body in Christ, and individually members one of another. Having gifts that differ according to the grace given to us, let us use them: if prophecy, in proportion to our faith; if service, in our serving; the one who teaches, in his teaching; the one who exhorts, in his exhortation; the one who contributes, in generosity; the one who leads, with zeal; the one who does acts of mercy, with cheerfulness.'

(Romans 12 vs 4-8 ESV)

ACCEPTANCE

Father God,

Help me to feel and be accepted for who I am. Help me to accept others for who they are too.

You know me by name and you love me – thank you, God.

Teach me and show me of your love and desire to know me. I give you my fears and worries, my situations and my life.

Help me to accept you and your ways, to treat everyone with respect and love, and do good in this world.

Thank you for forgiving me when I get things wrong, for your grace and mercy every day.

In Jesus' name.

Amen.

• • • • • • •

'I thank Christ Jesus our Lord, who has given me strength to do his work. He considered me trustworthy and appointed me to serve him, even though I used to blaspheme the name of Christ. In my insolence, I persecuted his people. But God had mercy on me because I did it in ignorance and unbelief.'

(1 Timothy 1 vs 12-13 NLT)

ACHIEVEMENT

Lord God,

Although there are many times when we have failed, teach us that this is ok.

Sometimes, however, we do really well and achieve. Today, we thank you for all of our achievements, however great or small.

Remind us that the greatest achievement of all is Jesus overcoming death on a cross.

Thank you that our sins have been taken away and we are a new creation in you.

You are the reason there is good; thank you, Jesus.

When I achieve, I praise you; when I fail, I praise you.

When others achieve, help us to celebrate with them too.

Amen.

'Observe the requirements of the LORD your God, and follow all his ways. Keep the decrees, commands, regulations, and laws written in the Law of Moses so that you will be successful in all you do and wherever you go.'

(1 Kings 2 vs 3 NLT)

ACTION

Lord God,

Thank you that you taught us to act on our faith and do good because you are good.

Help us to act properly, to do good in this world and be an example to others.

Sorry, Lord, that we don't always get it right and don't always act as we should.

Today, help us to be a people of action, shining a light in the world and bringing you glory.

Amen.

• • • • • • •

'What good is it, my brothers and sisters, if someone claims to have faith but has no deeds? Can such faith save them? Suppose a brother or a sister is without clothes and daily food. If one of you says to them, "Go in peace; keep warm and well fed," but does nothing about their physical needs, what good is it? In the same way, faith by itself, if it is not accompanied by action, is dead. But someone will say, "You have faith; I have deeds." Show me your faith without deeds, and I will show you my faith by my deeds. You believe that there is one God. Good! Even the demons believe that – and shudder. You foolish person, do you want evidence that faith without deeds is useless? Was not our father Abraham considered righteous for what he did when he offered his son Isaac on the altar? You see that his faith and his actions were working together, and his faith was made complete by what he did.'

(James 2 vs 14-22 NIV)

ADVENT

Come, Lord Jesus!

Open our lives to the peace, which you alone bring.

Let us turn to you, and be ready!

Amen.

'There shall come forth a shoot from the stump of Jesse, and a branch from his roots shall bear fruit. And the Spirit of the Lord shall rest upon him, the Spirit of wisdom and understanding, the Spirit of counsel and might, the Spirit of knowledge and the fear of the Lord. And his delight shall be in the fear of the Lord. He shall not judge by what his eyes see, or decide disputes by what his ears hear, but with righteousness he shall judge the poor, and decide with equity for the meek of the earth; and he shall strike the earth with the rod of his mouth, and with the breath of his lips he shall kill the wicked. Righteousness shall be the belt of his waist, and faithfulness the belt of his loins.'

(Isaiah 11 vs 1-5 ESV)

ADVENTURE

Dear God,

When we take risks and try something new, you are with us.

When we go on an adventure, you are beside us.

When we are scared to do a task and try something new, you help us.

When we feel alone and far from anyone, you walk with us.

Help us to enjoy life's many adventures, sharing in all of them with us.

In Jesus' name.

Amen.

'But thanks be to God, who always leads us as captives in Christ's triumphal procession and uses us to spread the aroma of the knowledge of him everywhere.'

(2 Corinthians 2 vs 14 NIV)

ADVICE

Dear Lord,

Guide our lives in your ways of truth and love, kindness and humility.

Help us to receive good advice from others graciously, and to use it wisely when we find ourselves at a crossroads, or in difficult situations.

Help us to share good counsel with others and advise well.

May we learn to trust in you and your word more and more every day!

Amen.

'Listen to advice and accept instruction, that you may gain wisdom in the future.'
(Proverbs 19 vs 20 ESV)

AMBITION

Ambition is the path to success. Persistence is the vehicle you arrive in.

Dear Lord,

Give me ambitions to be the best I can be, and grant me the desires of my heart.

Give me ambitions to help others be the best they can be.

Give us all ambitions to make this world a better place.

Give us ambitions to know you more, and to accept your will.

Give me ambitions to share your love with all.

Amen.

'Do nothing out of selfish ambition or vain conceit.
Rather, in humility value others above yourselves, not looking to your own interests but each of you to the interests of the others.'
(Philippians 2 vs 3-4 NIV)

Prayers for Schools

ANGER

Dear God,

We all get angry at times and this is normal. Help us to manage our anger wisely, so that it is not a hindrance to us, so the energy from anger can be used for good.

Take any hurt and upset we have in our lives, which might cause us to turn in anger quickly.

Give us patience where we are lacking. Lord, bring restoration to situations where anger has caused a break.

Finally, help me to trust you, Lord. Renew me from the inside. Forgive all my wrongdoings.

Thank you, Lord.

Amen.

'You shall not hate your brother in your heart, but you shall reason frankly with your neighbour, lest you incur sin because of him. You shall not take vengeance or bear a grudge against the sons of your own people, but you shall love your neighbour as yourself: I am the Lord.'

(Leviticus 19 vs 17-18 ESV)

ANXIETY

Lord God,

When I feel anxious about a situation, remind me that you are there with me.

Help me to overcome fear and worries and place my trust in you.

Help me to seek you in prayer when I feel anxious about anything, Lord.

Today, remind me that you are greater and more powerful than any anxiety I have.

When others feel anxious, give me the courage and wisdom to help and comfort them.

Amen.

'Do not be anxious about anything, but in everything, by prayer and petition, with thanksgiving, present your requests to God. And the peace of God, which transcends all understanding, will guard your hearts and your minds in Christ Jesus.'

(Philippians 4 vs 6-7 NIV)

AUTHORITY

Dear God,

We thank you, Lord, for those in authority over us at school: our headteacher, our year heads and our teachers. Thank you also for our parents and carers who love us, look after us and keep us safe.

We pray for our leaders and those in charge. Guide them to do the right thing, and help us to obey the rules that they put in place. Help us to follow your rules, Lord, and live godly lives. Let us look to the example Jesus set us in his life.

Let us remember the work of the police, the government and all those in authority over us. It is not an easy job and without these people, life would be a lot more difficult.

Finally, God, when we do wrong, forgive us; when we fall short of your expectations, help us; when we need comfort, draw close to us. Help us to respect authority, to do what is right and make us thankful for every blessing.

Amen.

'First of all, then, I urge that entreaties and prayers, petitions and thanksgivings, be made on behalf of all men, for kings and all who are in authority, so that we may lead a tranquil and quiet life in all godliness and dignity.'

(1 Timothy 2 vs 1-2)

AUTUMN

Dear Lord,

We thank you for the seasons, which mark the passing of time.

Autumn is such a beautiful time of year. As the trees surrender their leaves, help us to surrender our lives to you.

During this season, you remind us that sometimes things must die and fall away for new life to arise.

Such is the message of Jesus who died on the cross, that through death to self, we can find new life in him.

In moments when we experience setbacks and failures, help us to remember that you are always with us, God.

You are the God of life, you believe in us, you trust us, love us and yearn to be closer to us all.

Help us to trust in you and in your promise of new life, and help us to enjoy this very special season.

Amen.

'When I look at your heavens, the work of your fingers, the moon and the stars, which you have set in place.'
(Psalm 8 vs 3 ESV)

AWE

Dear Lord,

Wow! What a world you have created, what wonders you have made.

Let us today both marvel at creation and stand in awe of nature's beauty.

We thank you for this season – the plants, flowers, the wonderful wildlife and humankind.

Bless all key workers who serve and care for us. We stand in awe of them!

We thank you for sending Jesus, your only Son, so that we can have life in its fullness.

Help us to appreciate this beautiful world, to love it, protect it and respect it. Help us do the same for our fellow human beings too.

Amen.

'Everyone was filled with awe at the many wonders
and signs performed by the apostles.'
(Acts 2 vs 43 NIV)

'He himself bore our sins in his body on the tree, that we might die to sin and
live to righteousness. By his wounds you have been healed.'
(1 Peter 2 vs 24 ESV)

THE BEATITUDES

The beatitudes reveal some of God's standards of beauty.

It is being aware of one's spiritual poverty, sadness for wickedness, hunger and thirst for righteousness, mercy, purity of heart, and being a peacemaker.

Human attributes valued by God: keeping a living faith while enduring physical hardships, controlling the tongue, making sacrifices for the good of others, and living by Christian convictions in the face of ridicule.

All these are beautiful to God.

'Now faith is confidence in what we hope for and assurance about what we do not see.'

(Hebrews 11 vs 1 NIV)

BEAUTY

Dear Lord,

We thank you for all the beauty there is in our world.

We pray against all that spoils it – war, famine, poverty and suffering. Help us to change our world through prayer and action.

Thank you that you do not look at outward beauty, but you look to the heart and inner beauty.

Help us to focus on seeing others with your eyes and, Lord, change our hearts where we lack inner beauty.

God, thank you that you think of us all as beautiful, each and every one.

Help us to make this world a more beautiful place.

In Jesus' name.

Amen.

'Do not let your adorning be external – the braiding of hair and the putting on of gold jewellery, or the clothing you wear – but let your adorning be the hidden person of the heart with the imperishable beauty of a gentle and quiet spirit, which in God's sight is very precious.'

(1 Peter 3 vs 3-4 ESV)

BEGINNINGS

Dear God,

Thank you for new beginnings and new starts.

Help all of us do our best to work hard, make the most of what we have and achieve our goals.

Thank you for everything that we have: our families, friends, classmates and teachers.

We pray that we are proud of ourselves through our behaviour, our kindness towards others and our work in school.

Thank you for our parents and carers who love us and support us.

Bless us all, now and always.

Amen

'May he grant you your heart's desire and fulfil all your plans!'
(Psalm 20 vs 4 ESV)

BEING RESILIENT

Dear Lord God,

Teach us the value and importance of being resilient, and thank you for the challenges in life that help to build us up.

Thank you for the times when a lack of resources reminds us of the value of resourcefulness.

When people frustrate, distract and annoy us, teach us patience and forgiveness.

Thank you for individual challenges we face at school and in life. The path is often difficult, but the journey has a purpose and we will learn resilience along the way.

Thank you for moments where we can show courage and boldness in our lives, with your help.

Help us to live a meaningful life, not just one of comfort and ease. Thank you for your Word, teaching us to hold on to what is good and building resilience within us.

We pray you continue to help us through difficult times, and when we fail in school, our jobs, in any walk of life, remind us that we can learn from mistakes and become stronger for it.

We thank you, Lord.

Amen.

• • • • • • • •

'We are pressed on every side by troubles, but we are not crushed. We are perplexed, but not driven to despair. We are hunted down, but never abandoned by God. We get knocked down, but we are not destroyed.'

(2 Corinthians 4 vs 8-9 NLT)

BEING RESOURCEFUL

Dear Lord God,

Help us in this wasteful world to be more resourceful with all that we have and all that we are given.

Make us aware of our personal strengths, and help us to make the best of what we have in all situations.

Help us to be resourceful in our learning, making wise use of time, talent, energy and our minds.

Help us to take more responsibility for our own progress and learning in the classroom, and become more resilient to setbacks.

Teach us, Lord, to see value in objects and ideas, but most of all in people.

And finally, prompt us to repair, reduce, reuse, and recycle.

Amen.

'If any of you lacks wisdom, let him ask God, who gives generously to all without reproach, and it will be given him.'

(James 1 vs 5 ESV)

BELIEFS

Dear God,

We are what we believe.

Help us to respect others' rights to believe in what they choose.

Help us to show respect to everyone irrespective of their beliefs.

Make yourself known to us, God.

Holy Spirit, we invite you to teach us, guide us in all that we are and what we do.

For those who don't know what to believe, speak to their hearts and help them.

Amen.

• • • • • • • •

'I pray that the eyes of your heart may be enlightened in order that you may know the hope to which he has called you, the riches of his glorious inheritance in his holy people, and his incomparably great power for us who believe.'

(Ephesians 1 vs 18-19 NIV)

BELONGING

Lord God,

Teach us this day that we all belong to someone.

Thank you that you are always there for us, every moment of the day and night.

Bless our families and friends who make us feel like we belong, and those who care.

Thank you that we belong to you and we are yours.

For your love for us all, thank you, God.

In Jesus' name.

Amen.

'There is neither Jew nor Gentile, neither slave nor free, nor is there male and female, for you are all one in Christ Jesus.'

(Galatians 3 vs 28 NIV)

THE BIBLE

Dear Lord,

Thank you for the Bible, your Word, such an important, influential book, a library of books, reminding us that you love us and want a relationship with each and every one of us.

Thank you God that your word is a manual for life, guiding us into truth and the right way.

Father, we thank you for Jesus who came, lived your words, gave his life for us, showed us how to live and taught us how to understand the message inside these pages.

Thank you for books; for words, communication, for messages, creative thoughts, inspiring poems that bring us life, happiness, reality, truth, fiction and more.

Help us to enjoy books, and realise what a blessing they are to us.

In Jesus' name.

Amen.

'In the beginning was the Word, and the Word was with God, and the Word was God.'

(John 1 vs 1 NIV)

'And we also thank God constantly for this, that when you received the word of God, which you heard from us, you accepted it not as the word of men but as what it really is, the word of God, which is at work in you believers.'

(1 Thessalonians 2 vs 13 ESV)

BODY

Dear God,

Thank you that you are a creator God who created humans.

Thank you that your breath started life.

Thank you that you love each one of us intimately and you know us by name.

Help us to look after our bodies; what we eat and drink, how we exercise and what we do with it.

Help us to look upon humans and see the beauty of your work in each one of them.

Help us to appreciate difference and praise you for every living being.

Holy Spirit, live within us, we pray.

Amen.

'For you formed my inward parts; you knitted me together in my mother's womb.'
(Psalm 139 vs 13-14 ESV)

'For we are God's masterpiece. He has created us anew in Christ Jesus, so we can do the good things he planned for us long ago.'
(Ephesians 2 vs 10 NLT)

BRAVERY

Dear Lord Jesus,

There will be times in our life when we will face great challenges: help us to be brave.

There will be times when we encounter sad situations or go through troubling times: help us to be brave.

When we face an uncertain future or suffer a loss, help us to be brave.

When we see others going through difficulty, help us comfort and support them.

Be with us in every situation, in every moment and with us every step of the way.

Amen.

'Wait patiently for the LORD. Be brave and courageous. Yes, wait patiently for the LORD.'
(Psalm 27 vs 14 NLT)

BULLYING

Bullying is the use of force, threat or coercion to abuse, intimidation or aggression used to impose domination over others. The behaviour is often repeated and habitual.

Dear Lord,

Let us all remember that when we laugh at someone, they feel pain.

Let us all remember that when we pick on someone, they are angry and afraid.

Let us all remember that when we do not stick up for someone who is being bullied, they are alone.

Let us all remember that bullies bully because they want to feel strong and in charge. This is so sad and wrong!

Remind us all to do what is right and to stop doing wrong.

Remind us all to show kindness and friendship to the lonely.

Remind us to tell an adult when we see any form of bullying, and to stand up against wrongdoing.

Finally, Lord, help us in these things that our school and community may become a better place for all.

In Jesus' name.

Amen.

• • • • • • •

'Be strong and courageous. Do not fear or be in dread of them, for it is the LORD your God who goes with you. He will not leave you or forsake you.'

(Deuteronomy 31 vs 6 ESV)

CALM

Lord Jesus,

In the storms of life, help me to be calm.

In difficult times, help me to surrender to you.

When the future looks bleak, help me to fully trust you.

When I feel overwhelmed, give me stillness.

Calm the storms in this world for the sake of your people and your glory.

Amen.

'Peace I leave with you; my peace I give to you. Not as the world gives do I give to you. Let not your hearts be troubled, neither let them be afraid.'

(John 14 vs 27 ESV)

CARE

Dear God,

Thank you for this wonderful world that you have made and all the people, animals and the plants.

Help us to respect each other, care for what we have and remember what you have done for us.

Thank you that you are always there for us, and you help us through all situations in life.

We pray for all the care homes, hospitals, respite centres and retreats in our community and across our county. Thank you that we are able to support each other in many ways.

Look after all the people who work in these settings and in our schools across the country.

Amen.

'Look not every man on his own things,
but every man also on the things of others.'
(Philippians 2 vs 4 KJV)

CELEBRATION

Dear God,

Thank you for moments of celebration.

Rejoice with us as we feel joy, pride and positive emotions.

Remind us to think of what you have done for us and celebrate this in our lives.

Helps us to be kind winners and good losers.

Finally, help us to be humble in victory and modest in life.

We celebrate Jesus' victory on the cross, today and every day.

Thank you, Lord.

Amen.

'Though you have not seen him, you love him. Though you do not now see him, you believe in him and rejoice with joy that is inexpressible and filled with glory, obtaining the outcome of your faith, the salvation of your souls.'

(1 Peter 1 vs 8-9 ESV)

CHANGES

Dear God,

Remind us that no matter what changes in our lives, you remain the same, always.

Help us all to prepare for changes, which are on the horizon: moving into a new Year group, starting a new school, working with new people.

Give us the strength to embrace change rather than fear it.

Lord, give us hope, the confidence and the tools to accept change, or to be the change.

Amen.

• • • • • • • •

'Every good gift and every perfect gift is from above, coming down from the Father of lights, with whom there is no variation or shadow due to change.'

(James 1 vs 17 ESV)

'The Lord is my rock and my fortress and my deliverer, my God, my rock, in whom I take refuge, my shield, and the horn of my salvation, my stronghold.'

(Psalm 18 vs 2 ESV)

CHARACTER/REPUTATION

Dear Lord,

Purify our hearts, minds and souls this week. Renew in us goodness and give us beautiful character, like Jesus.

Help us to be a light in our sometimes-dark world.

Renew a spirit of kindness in us and help us to make right choices.

Be there with us to weather life's storms, and help us to help others.

Let our virtues be bound with our reputations, so that we focus on doing good.

Thank you, Lord.

Amen.

'Therefore, my beloved, as you have always obeyed, so now, not only as in my presence but much more in my absence, work out your own salvation with fear and trembling, for it is God who works in you, both to will and to work for his good pleasure. Do all things without grumbling or disputing, that you may be blameless and innocent, children of God without blemish in the midst of a crooked and twisted generation, among whom you shine as lights in the world, holding fast to the word of life, so that in the day of Christ I may be proud that I did not run in vain or labour in vain.'

(Philippians 2 vs 12-16 ESV)

CHARITY

Dear God,

Thank you for charities and all the work and good they do.

Help us to be charitable in nature, helping those less fortunate than ourselves.

Help us to remember that we can be charitable with not just our money or items we don't need anymore, but with the time we can offer, a helping hand or a simple conversation, message or letter.

Please provide for those with nothing, for the hungry and those with no home.

Amen.

'Remember this: whoever sows sparingly will also reap sparingly, and whoever sows generously will also reap generously. Each of you should give what you have decided in your heart to give, not reluctantly or under compulsion, for God loves a cheerful giver.'

(2 Corinthians 9 vs 6-7 NIV)

CHOICES

Father God,

Today, we pray for help to make the right choices.

Today we make a decision and choose to do the right thing, do our best and be our best.

Help us to make wise choices, God, in the face of adversity and with self-control.

Give us the strength to follow through and be proud of good decisions.

Guide us in your ways, God, so that we might be successful and respected.

Today, help us to stand firm as honest, hard-working, trustworthy and dependable citizens.

In Jesus' name.

Amen.

'Wise choices will watch over you. Understanding will keep you safe.'
(Proverbs 2 vs 11 NLT)

CHRISTMAS

Dear God,

We thank you for this amazing time of year, when we celebrate the birth of our Lord Jesus.

Throughout the festive season, joyful or otherwise, let us remember we can turn to you, God, in prayer.

We pray for people who go without at Christmas or who are sad. Please provide for them, Lord, even if it means we are to provide for them.

We pray for our families and friends, that they have a fun-filled and happy time.

In this time of joy, song and laughter, we praise you for the great wonders you have sent us; the Word made flesh for us, in the little Child Jesus. We praise him like the three wise men and the lowly shepherds. Come to us, please Lord!

Finally, let us remember that Christmas is more about giving than receiving. Help us to be generous; to bring peace and love to everyone we meet. Help us be shining lights!

In Jesus' name.

Amen.

'Every good gift and every perfect gift is from above, coming down from the Father of lights with whom there is no variation or shadow due to change.'

(James 1 vs 17 ESV)

COMFORT

Dear God,

Bring us comfort today and all those times when we need picking up, or when we feel sad, alone or we are just having a bad day.

We thank you that your Holy Spirit is with each one of us, he is a comforter and all we need to do is call his name.

May we be a comfort to those around us, those who are far away or those we know who need cheering up.

Thank you for never leaving us, for always being available and for being a great comfort to us always.

Amen.

'But I will send you the Advocate – the Spirit of truth.
He will come to you from the Father and will testify all about me.'
(John 15 vs 26 NLT)

COMMITMENT

Dear Lord,

Thank you that each of our lives has purpose and meaning.

Thank you that the Bible says we are wonderfully made; help us to realise our worth to you and our family and friends.

When we are lacking in confidence, bring others into our lives who will build us up.

Finally, help us to trust in you at all times and know we are loved.

Amen.

'A new commandment I give to you, that you love one another: just as I have loved you, you also are to love one another. By this all people will know that you are my disciples, if you have love for one another.'

(John 13 vs 34-35 ESV)

Prayers for Schools

COMMON SENSE

Lord,

Help us to have sound judgement on practical matters.

Teach us discretion and prudence.

Give us wisdom to learn from experiences of positive outcomes and failures.

Help us to develop good common sense by learning from the consequences of our decision-making.

Above all, we seek your wisdom and understanding, Lord, in all things.

When we make mistakes, forgive us.

When we get things right, we give you thanks.

Amen.

'Good sense is a fountain of life to him who has it, but the instruction of fools is folly.'

(Proverbs 16 vs 22 ESV)

COMMUNICATION

Father God,

Help me today to properly listen to you with ears wide open.

Help me do the same with my family, friends and anyone I meet.

Give me the right words to say when I speak.

Help me to show good body language too.

In all my communication, through my actions and words, may I be a blessing to you.

Help me to speak words of compassion, kindness and generosity today, so that others may be blessed too.

In Jesus' name.

Amen.

'Let your speech always be gracious, seasoned with salt, so that you may know how you ought to answer each person.'
(Colossians 4 vs 6 ESV)

COMMUNITY

Dear God,

Thank you for the community we live in and for all the many people who make it what it is.

Thank you for our school, our community and the great people who work and study here.

Today we ask for a blessing for or all those in our town and the wider community.

Remind each one of us of your love, give us your comfort when we feel down and keep us safe, Lord.

Be with us all, Jesus, everyone linked to our school; all the children, staff, trustees (our governors) and parents, guardians and carers.

Hear our prayer today and speak to us in our quiet moments.

Hold us close this day God, and help each one of us shine a light in our community that we might bless others.

Amen.

'Finally, all of you, be like-minded, be sympathetic, love one another, be compassionate and humble.'

(1 Peter 3 vs 8 NIV)

'But if we walk in the light, as he is in the light, we have fellowship with one another, and the blood of Jesus, his Son, purifies us from all sin.'

(1 John 1 vs 7 ESV)

COMPASSION

Dear Lord,

Teach us how to be compassionate, caring and thoughtful.

Help us to reach out to others less fortunate than ourselves and be thankful for what we do have.

God, help us to forgive each other as Jesus forgave us.

Help us to show compassion to each other in our school and in our wider community, putting others first wherever we go.

Thank you, Jesus.

Amen.

'Therefore, as God's chosen people, holy and dearly loved, clothe yourselves with compassion, kindness, humility, gentleness and patience.'

(Colossians 3 vs 12 NIV)

COMPROMISE

Lord Jesus,

Help me commit fully to your ways and not compromise an inch.

Holy Spirit, give me the strength to live a holy life, as best I can, and praise you.

Help me to follow your advice and word in the Bible, so that I can live my best life.

In life, when a compromise is needed in coming to an agreement, help me to make wise decisions.

Lead me, God, today, help me to stand firm on principles and values and keep me from wrongdoing.

Amen.

'A servant of the Lord must not quarrel but must be kind to everyone, be able to teach, and be patient with difficult people.'
(2 Timothy 2 vs 24 NLT)

CONDUCT

Dear Lord,

Sometimes my behaviour is not what it should be and for that I am sorry.

Please help me to improve the way I treat others and help me to think about the consequences of my actions.

Jesus, you set an example to us all of how to live a good life, putting others first, being caring and considerate towards others. Help me to be more like you in my own life.

Lord, let my conduct be an example to others and may I be a blessing to you, and all who I meet.

For your glory.

Amen.

'You shall love the Lord your God with all your heart and with all your soul and with all your strength and with all your mind, and your neighbour as yourself.'

(Luke 10 vs 27 ESV)

CONFIDENCE (in Jesus)

Dear Lord,

Thank you for the many blessings you have given us in our lives.

Help us to be grateful and to remember those who are lacking in basic needs at this time.

Provide us with opportunities to share your love and hope to all we meet.

Thank you that you always stand beside us and offer us a future full of your love, blessings and guidance.

Your Word says that no matter how bad things get, you will always be right beside us. We may not see you, we may not feel you, but we thank you, Lord, for giving us your Word that tells us you are here.

God, you know our dreams. Search our hearts, Lord, and hear our prayers of hope.

We trust you with our dreams for you are a God who answers prayer. Thank you for the hope we have in you!

Help us to trust in you more and more every day, God.

Amen.

'Faith shows the reality of what we hope for;
it is the evidence of things we cannot see.'
(Hebrews 11 vs 1 NLT)

CONSCIENCE

An inner feeling or voice viewed as acting as a guide to the rightness or wrongness of one's behaviour.

Dear Lord,

Speak to us in those times when we do wrong and help us to do what is right.

Holy Spirit, guide us in your ways and prompt us when we make mistakes. Prick our conscience in order that we might make the right decisions in all walks of life.

Help us to think of those less fortunate than ourselves, that we might reach out to them, support them and befriend them.

Jesus, help us to live more like you, become more aware of our behaviour, and begin to actively make a more positive impact in others' lives.

God, we ask you to help us to be more honest, so that we can have a clear conscience and we can be who you want us to be.

In Jesus' name,

Amen.

'If we confess our sins, he is faithful and just to forgive us our sins and to cleanse us from all unrighteousness.'

(1 John 1 vs 9 ESV)

CONSERVATION

Dear God,

Help us to respect, protect and care for our environment, so that others can enjoy it.

Help us to appreciate and enjoy the beauty of nature and the countryside and do our best to conserve it for future generations.

God, help us to think of new ways to protect the environment, and be more sustainable through recycling and reducing the amount we waste.

Lord, help us to be good stewards of the environment, look after it, respect it, enjoy it and even improve it.

We remember that everything on earth is yours; thank you for it, Lord.

Amen.

'The earth is the LORD's, and everything in it.'

(Psalm 24 vs 1 NIV)

CONSIDERATION

Dear God,

Be with us as we work today. Fill this school with inspiration and energy.

Help all the pupils and staff to work as a team and bring out the best in each other.

May we be efficient and achieve well, and remember to rest when we need to.

Help us to create a school full of fun and friendship as well as hard work and harmony. Let us always be considerate of one another.

Thank you for the opportunity to work together and learn from one another; this is what makes community.

Amen.

'Two are better than one, because they have a good reward for their toil. For if they fall, one will lift up his fellow.'
(Ecclesiastes 4 vs 9-10 ESV)

CO-OPERATION

Dear God,

Be with us as we work today. Fill our school with inspiration, focus and energy.

Help all the pupils at this school to work as a team, and bring out the best in each other.

May we be efficient and achieve well, but also remember to rest when we need to.

May this school be full of fun and friendship as well as hard work and harmony.

Thank you for the opportunity to work together, learn from one another and cooperate.

Amen.

'Two are better than one, because they have a good reward for their toil. For if they fall, one will lift up his fellow.'

(Ecclesiastes 4 vs 9-10 ESV)

COURAGE

Dear God,

Give us courage and wisdom to always do what is right.

Forgive us when we get things wrong!

Give us the strength to stand up for what is right and the courage to stand alone against wrong.

Let our behaviour and morals be a blessing to you and others.

We thank you for those in authority who dedicate their lives to make us safe, happy and successful.

In Jesus' name.

Amen.

'If we confess our sins, he is faithful and just to forgive us our sins and to cleanse us from all unrighteousness.'

(1 John 1 vs 9 ESV)

CREATION

Dear Lord,

Thank you for creation this day: the earth, the sky, the sea and everything in it.

We praise you for the vastness of the universe and beyond.

And we thank you for your love for each one of us.

Help us to respect and care for all of your creation, and be good stewards on earth.

Amen.

• • • • • • • •

'In the beginning God created the heaven and the earth. And the earth was without form, and void; and darkness was upon the face of the deep. And the Spirit of God moved upon the face of the waters.'

(Genesis 1 vs 1-2 KJV)

CREATIVITY

Dear Lord,

Thank you for creativity and for wonderful, intelligent people who create.

We are made in your image, God, to be creative, but we won't always get it right the first time.

Give us the perseverance and humility to deal with failure well, so that we pick ourselves up and use failure to move us on to greater things.

Thank you, God, for those who have failed before us yet have carried on, beyond their disappointment, to create brilliant things.

We praise you for their dedication and commitment. Help us all to be like them!

Amen.

'For we are his workmanship, created in Christ Jesus for good works, which God prepared beforehand, that we should walk in them.'

(Ephesians 2 vs 10 ESV)

DARKNESS

Holy Spirit,

When the earth was void and formless and dark, you spoke your light and power and love into it.

In any darkness others or we have, bring your light, power and love today.

Remind us that the darkness is powerless, it is weak and there is nothing to fear.

Be with us in those times in our lives when we will go through difficulties and distress.

Help us be a light in our school, community and world, spreading goodness wherever we go.

Help us to see the truth in your Word in the Bible and begin to live out your commands.

Thank you, Lord.

Amen.

'For you are my lamp, O Lord, and my God lightens my darkness.'

(2 Samuel 22 vs 29 ESV)

DIFFERENCES

Dear God,

Thank you for kind friends, for smiley and encouraging teachers. Thank you for our pets that we love.

We are grateful that each of us has a personality, unique and individual, that makes us what we are.

Help us to appreciate the variety of personalities and the mix of characters we have in our school- it is what makes our community and school an interesting, special place and the reason why meeting new people and making new friends is fun!

Help us to develop our good nature, the caring side to our being where kindness rules.

Lord, help us be our best and shine! Help us to celebrate difference, giving you the glory for the uniqueness and beauty of your creation.

Amen.

'But the LORD said to Samuel, "Do not look on his appearance or on the height of his stature, because I have rejected him. For the LORD sees not as man sees: man looks on the outward appearance, but the LORD looks on the heart."'

(1 Samuel 16 vs 7 ESV)

DIFFICULTIES

Holy Spirit,

When we face difficulties today, be with us and help us to overcome them.

When we face hardship in life, help us to remain calm and do the right thing.

When we see others in difficulty, may we be a help to them and offer support.

When we each overcome difficulties, remind us to praise you.

In good times and bad, Lord, we thank you and praise you.

Amen.

'And we know that for those who love God all things work together for good, for those who are called according to his purpose.'

(Romans 8 vs 28 ESV)

DISAPPOINTMENT

Dear God,

There will be times in our lives when we will all face disappointment of some kind. Help us to overcome these difficult times and to trust in you.

Lord, strengthen the spirit within us and bring your comfort.

For those currently facing disappointment, help us to comfort them.

When we face similar circumstances, prepare us and give us renewed hope.

Lord, we seek you in times of trouble; our refuge and strength.

We pray open and honestly to you for support, guidance and love.

Amen.

'Weeping may last through the night, but joy comes with the morning.'
(Psalm 30 vs 5 NLT)

DISCOVERY

Father God,

The greatest discovery we could ever make in this world is you.

Lord, speak to us and open our ears to your words.

Help us to discover you in the beauty and wonder of nature, and in the words and deeds of people.

Help us to find in you what we truly need – a saviour, a friend, a Lord of our life.

Finally, God, help us to be good role models in the way we live our lives, and be more like Jesus.

In your holy name.

Amen.

'Call to me and I will answer you, and will tell you great and hidden things that you have not known.'
(Jeremiah 33 vs 3 ESV)

DREAMS

An end-of-year school prayer.

Dear Lord Jesus,

Help us to remember the special memories we have created this past year as a community.

Help us to put what we have learned to good use in the future, so that we are able to follow and realise our dreams.

Thank you for this year, for the community we have been a part of and for the amazing achievements of us all.

Help us to use this summer and the next academic year, this September, as a platform for greater things in the next phase of our school journey.

Thank you for all the hard-working staff, our parents and carers, and all the people who have helped us on our way.

May our summer break be a time of rest and refreshing, a time to reflect and dream. And, please continue to guide us, Lord.

In Jesus' name.

Amen.

'Do not be anxious about anything, but in everything by prayer and supplication with thanksgiving let your requests be made known to God.'
(Philippians 4 vs 6 ESV)

DUTY

Dear Father God,

My duty is to love you, walk in your ways and serve you with all my heart, mind and soul.

Help me to achieve that with perseverance, humbleness, passion and strength.

We thank you for our parents, guardians and teachers who have a duty of care to us. May we show our appreciation and thankfulness in our words and deeds to all those who care, protect and keep us safe.

Those people on duty, serving in the army, police force, fire service, doctors, nurses and all care workers; bless them for the service they provide. Help us to remember them now, especially anyone we know, as we pray.

Lord Jesus, help us to focus on our duty at school to work hard and be the best we can be in our learning, in our friendships, and how we speak to and treat others.

Help us to understand your ways, God, by learning more about you in the Bible and from Christians.

Amen.

• • • • • • •

'Fear God and keep his commandments, for this is the whole duty of man. For God will bring every deed into judgment, with every secret thing, whether good or evil.'

(Ecclesiastes 12 vs 13-14 ESV)

EARTH

Dear Lord,

As we think about our planet, Father God, help us to care for all that you have given us.

Thank you for all life and for the abundance of good things that we have.

Make us aware of how delicate these things are, and help us to preserve, protect and promote all things by being good stewards, thinking about both the actions and the choices we can make in the world in which we live.

Lord, help us to look after our wildlife, nature and the environment. Help us also to treat people well, be less greedy and to share more.

Help us to solve the issues, which cause conflict and stress in so many places around the world, so that earth can be a more peaceful place to live.

We ask for these things in Jesus' name.

Amen.

'Working the land is crucial for human flourishing – but guarding the earth is the critical complement.'
(Jewish Teaching)

EASTER

Almighty God,

We remember all that you did at the cross, your life given up for us.

We thank you that you had compassion and kindness on your people and you loved us so much you sent Jesus to die in our place.

This Easter time, we celebrate how you overcame death and sin and conquered the grave.

You are our hope, the way, the truth and the life.

Thank you.

Amen.

'Jesus answered, "I am the way and the truth and the life. No one comes to the Father except through me."'

(John 14 vs 6 NIV)

ELDERLY

Father God,

Thank you for the elderly with all their experience and wisdom.

Make us thankful for relatives and friends who are elderly; may we care for them and show them the respect they deserve.

We ask for good health and happiness for all those in later years.

For the poor, sick and lonely, please provide all they need, God.

Amen.

'Wisdom belongs to the aged, and understanding to the old.'
(Job 12 vs 12 NLT)

EMPATHY

The ability to understand and share the feelings of another.

Lord,

In a world where we all have difficulties in our lives, help us to show empathy and compassion towards others around us going through a hard time.

We ask for the grace and strength to be people of empathy – people who can really identify with and feel the concerns of those around us.

Today, make me thankful for every blessing in my life, but help me to be considerate of others too.

Help us to see situations from another person's point of view, to listen when people speak and to notice when someone is upset. Jesus, help us to comfort others and give sound advice.

Lord, teach me to be more empathetic, supportive and kind.

Today and always.

Amen.

'Rejoice with those who rejoice, weep with those who weep.'
(Romans 12 vs 15 ESV)

'Finally, all of you, have unity of mind, sympathy, brotherly love, a tender heart, and a humble mind.'
(1 Peter 3 vs 8 ESV)

END OF SCHOOL YEAR

Dear Lord Jesus,

Help us to remember our time at school with teachers and friends and all the special memories we have created this past year.

Help us to use what we have learned and put it to good use in the future.

Thank you for this year, for the community we have been a part of at this school and for the achievements of all. We are so fortunate to be part of such a wonderful school, so help us to use this year as a platform for greater things in the next phase of our school journey.

Thank you for all the hard-working staff, the parents and carers and all the people who have helped us on our way. May our summer break be a time of rest and refreshment, a time to reflect and dream.

Please continue to guide us, Lord.

Amen.

'Trust in the Lord with all your heart, and do not lean on your own understanding. In all your ways acknowledge him, and he will make straight your paths.'

(Proverbs 3 vs 5-6 ESV)

ENDURANCE

Dear Lord,

Today I ask for strength and endurance to get through this day and this week.

Holy Spirit, fill me this day and walk beside me as I navigate the ups and downs of life.

Help me to support those of us who are struggling and help lift them up spiritually.

Amen.

'Fear not, for I am with you; be not dismayed, for I am your God; I will strengthen you, I will help you, I will uphold you with my righteous right hand.'
(Isaiah 41 vs 10 ESV)

ENEMIES

Dear Lord,

Your word tells us to pray for our enemies and to love our enemies which is quite a challenge.

Help us, God, to resolve conflict with those we fall out with, and to forgive wrongdoings against us.

Guide us in your ways and protect us, Lord.

Help us to speak well, show humility, kindness, gentleness and respect to all people.

Help all of us in our school to be shining lights in our community.

When others fail to forgive us for any wrongs we have done, we pray that you will break down the barriers and bring a light into their lives.

Let there be harmony not discord in our school, community and town.

In Jesus' name.

Amen.

'But I say to you who hear, Love your enemies, do good to those who hate you, bless those who curse you, pray for those who abuse you.'

(Luke 6 vs 27-28 ESV)

ENJOYMENT/FUN

Dear Lord Jesus,

Thank you for the opportunity that play and recreation bring; the fun and enjoyment, the learning and the time to rest.

Make us thankful, Lord, for the opportunities afforded us in this country – how blessed we are!

Help us to make the most of the opportunities we are given at school, in our home and in our communities.

Help us to try different activities, learn and develop new skills, so that we may make new friends and discover more about ourselves.

Finally, we thank you for all the staff at school, and those people who enable us to take part in these activities, who give their time and support to teach us.

Renew us today, Lord, and help us to enjoy this week.

Thank you, God.

Amen.

'And whatever you do, in word or deed, do everything in the name of the Lord Jesus, giving thanks to God the Father.'

(Colossians 3 vs 17 ESV)

ENVIRONMENT

Dear God,

Thank you for the wonderful grounds we have in our school and for the people who look after them for us.

Help us to respect, protect and care for our environment. Help us to appreciate and enjoy the beauty of nature and the countryside, and to also consider our environment at school.

God, help us to think of new ways to protect the environment in more sustainable ways through recycling and reducing the amount we waste.

Finally, Lord, help us to be good stewards of the environment, to look after it, respect it and enjoy it.

Amen.

'You alone are the LORD. You made the heavens, even the highest heavens, and all their starry host, the earth and all that is on it, the seas and all that is in them. You give life to everything, and the multitudes of heaven worship you.'

(Nehemiah 9 vs 6 NIV)

'The earth is the LORD's, and everything in it.'

(Psalm 24 vs 1 NIV)

EPIPHANY*

1. A Christian festival, observed on January 6, which commemorates the arrival of the wise men soon after Jesus' birth.
2. An appearance or manifestation, especially of a deity.
3. A sudden insight into the reality or essential meaning of something, usually initiated by some occurrence or experience.
4. A literary work or section of a work presenting, usually symbolically, such a moment of revelation and insight.

A NEW YEAR PRAYER

by W. E. Orchard, 1877–1955

Grant us grace, O God,
to begin this year in your faith
and to continue it in your favour,
that being guided in all our doings
and guarded all our days,
we may spend ourselves in your service
and finally, by your grace,
attain to the glory of eternal life;
through Christ our Lord.
Amen.

*The Magi Visit the Messiah (Matthew 2 vs 1-12)

EXAMPLE

Dear God,

Help me to love my neighbour as I do myself and to be a good example.

Help me to treat every human with dignity, respect and love.

Help me to speak up for the poor, the weak, the lonely and the oppressed.

Help me to be merciful to others in my life.

Thank you, Lord, for the example of Jesus.

Amen.

'In everything set them an example by doing what is good.
In your teaching show integrity, seriousness.'

(Titus 2 vs 7 NIV)

FAILING WELL

Dear Lord Jesus,

When I give my all in everything I do, I will at times still fail. This is inevitability part of life for everyone on God's earth.

Help me to realise that any failure is quite simply the first steps to success. When we were toddlers, we fell hundreds of times before we learned how to walk. Help me to fail and fall graciously.

In life, when I come across failure, remind me to be resilient and not give up; help me to turn negatives into positives and dismay into hope.

When others around me fail, let me be an encouragement to them to try and try again, until they succeed.

Amen.

'So do not fear, for I am with you; do not be dismayed, for I am your God.
I will strengthen you and help you;
I will uphold you with my righteous right hand.'

(Isaiah 41 vs 10 NIV)

FAITH

Dear Lord,

Today, help us to have a deeper faith in you.

Help us to realise who you are and what you have done for us.

As we come to know you more by speaking to you and reading your word, help us to share that with others and grow in stature and strength and confidence in the knowledge of your truth.

May our lives praise you and may we be a blessing to whomever we meet.

Thank you that you always stand beside us- your word says that no matter how bad things get, you will always be right beside us.

You know our dreams. Search our hearts, Lord, and hear our prayers of hope. We trust you and thank you for the hope we have in you!

In your name, Jesus.

Amen.

• • • • • • •

'And Jesus answered them, "Have faith in God. Truly, I say to you, whoever says to this mountain, 'Be taken up and thrown into the sea', and does not doubt in his heart, but believes that what he says will come to pass, it will be done for him. Therefore I tell you, whatever you ask in prayer, believe that you have received it, and it will be yours.'"

(Mark 11 vs 22-24 ESV)

FAITHFULNESS

The quality of being faithful

Dear Jesus,

Thank you for being a faithful friend.

Help us to put our trust in you each day.

Thank you for never giving up on us, for always loving us and for dying on a cross for our sins.

Help us to mirror your faithfulness in our lives, in our relationships and in our work.

Teach us the importance of obeying your commands.

Help us to resist temptations and wrongdoing, so that we live the best life possible.

Thank you for those people we know who stick by us even when we upset and hurt them.

Help us to do the same; forgive freely, remain faithful always and love others.

In your name we pray.

Amen.

• • • • • • •

'I no longer count on my own righteousness through obeying the law; rather, I become righteous through faith in Christ. For God's way of making us right with himself depends on faith.'

(Philippians 3 vs 9 NLT)

FAMILY

Dear Lord Jesus,

Thank you for our families, for all they do for us and all that they mean to us.

Help us to appreciate what our parents, grandparents, brothers, sisters, aunties and uncles do for us.

May the love that binds our own, unique family situation grow daily. Help us to forgive each other quickly when we feel we have been wronged.

We thank you for foster families, guardians and carers too, for all they do to create and be a family for the young people in their care; bless them richly, Lord.

Help us at all times to treat each other like family, with care, respect and kindness, just like you did, Jesus.

Thank you that you draw close to us when we are down and rejoice with us when we are happy.

We ask these things in your name.

Amen.

'Honour your father and your mother, that your days may be long in the land that the LORD your God is giving you.'

(Exodus 20 vs 12 ESV)

'For where your treasure is, your heart will be also.'

(Luke 12 vs 34 NIV)

FEAR

Dear Father,

When my heart and mind are flooded with fears, sometimes I feel unable to go on. These fears are overwhelming.

Instead, I hold onto your truth. You have told us not to fear, for you have overcome even death itself.

I cling to you; I trust in your promises, that you will never fail me and never abandon me.

In moments of such crippling fear, hold my hand. I know you have experienced the most fearful places and I know that you overcome your fears.

Let this be a reminder that I, too, can overcome fear with courage and determination.

Amen.

• • • • • • •

'The fear of man lays a snare, but whoever trusts in the Lord is safe.'
(Proverbs 29 vs 25 ESV)

'Do not be anxious about anything, but in everything by prayer and supplication with thanksgiving let your requests be made known to God.'
(Philippians 4 vs 6 ESV)

FLOODS/BARRIERS

Dear God,

We pray for all those affected by floods around the world and for all those who will be affected in the future. As people try to restore homes, businesses and their lives, bring communities together.

We pray that those in authority now build the barriers needed to stop future floods causing so much devastation in the future. Give them wisdom Lord!

We pray for support for those who need it, through prayers, acts of kindness and offerings of goodwill.

Finally, help us all to lower our barriers to allow more of you in our lives.

Holy Spirit, flood us with your compassion, kindness and love. Bring our barriers down.

Help each one of us be a beacon in the community and in our world, a true example of your selfless love for us.

In Jesus' name.

Amen.

'And your ancient ruins shall be rebuilt; you shall raise up the foundations of many generations; you shall be called the repairer of the breach, the restorer of streets to dwell in.'

(Isaiah 58 vs 12 ESV)

FOCUS

Dear Lord God,

Through the darkest times often our focus becomes much clearer and we see the light.

Help me today to focus on what is important, on what is right and what is good.

May I focus on you this week, and beyond, on being the best I can be and to help others.

In times of darkness, let us see your light.

Let me be a light for others too, a ray of sunshine in their day.

Be praised this day, Lord, as we focus on you and your Word.

Amen.

'I focus on this one thing: forgetting the past and looking forward to what lies ahead, I press on to reach the end of the race and receive the heavenly prize for which God, through Christ Jesus, is calling us.'

(Philippians 3 vs 13-14 NLT)

'See how far you can go and go as far as you can see.'

(Anonymous)

FORGIVENESS

Dear Lord,

Thank you for your forgiveness, your mercy and your grace each and every day.

Give us courage and wisdom to always do what is right. Forgive us when we get things wrong!

Give us the strength to stand up for what is right and the courage to stand alone if necessary. Let our behaviour and morals bless you.

Help us this day to forgive all those who have wronged us.

Give us the strength to say sorry and make amends.

We ask that you make today a day of healing and restoration.

As you forgave us, we forgive others today and move on.

In your holy name.

Amen.

'Bearing with one another and, if one has a complaint against another, forgiving each other; as the Lord has forgiven you, so you also must forgive.'

(Colossians 3 vs 13 ESV)

FRIENDS

Dear God,

We thank you for the gift and beauty of friendship.

We thank you for our friends and all they do for us, how they make us feel and how they are a light in our lives.

We pray for those without friends, the lonely, the helpless and the persecuted. Provide for them a comfort, Lord.

Thank you, Jesus, that we have a friend in you. Thank you that you are always there for us, always willing to listen to us and always there to advise us in your Word.

Help us all to be an honest, trustworthy and supportive friend.

Be with our friends today, their families and our distant loved ones.

Help us to understand the importance of friendship, to be a good friend by keeping in touch, writing, emailing, and phoning each other to show we care.

Friends are wonderful; we thank you for them, Lord.

Amen

'A friend loves at all times.'
(Proverbs 17 vs 17 NIV)

'Snowflakes are one of nature's most fragile things, but just look at what they can do when they stick together.'
(Vesta Kelly)

FRIENDSHIP

Dear God,

Thank you for our friends and family, and thank you so much for friendship, a true gift and something very beautiful.

Help us to cherish the relationships we have with family, friends and people we know. Help us to be kind to all we meet.

Lord, help us to build strong, lasting friendships through mutual trust and kindness, respect, care and love.

When we face difficulties in our relationships, God, give us all the strength, patience and grace we need.

Help us to care for everyone around us, whether they are our friends or not.

Thank you that Jesus is our friend and we can pray to him and share our worries in life.

Help me be the best friend I can be, and offer the hand of friendship to new people I meet.

Amen.

• • • • • • •

'Two are better than one, because they have a good reward for their toil.
For if they fall, one will lift up his fellow. But woe to him who is alone
when he falls and has not another to lift him up! Again, if two lie together,
they keep warm, but how can one keep warm alone?
And though a man might prevail against one who is alone,
two will withstand him – a threefold cord is not quickly broken.'

(Ecclesiastes 4 vs 9-12 ESV)

GENEROSITY

Dear Lord,

Thank you that you are a generous God.

Give me an opportunity this day and over the weekend to be generous to someone else.

Today I give you thanks for every blessing in my life.

Like you, help me be a blessing to others and bring some joy.

Thank you for generous people, how they are appreciated.

Help me to give something back to them.

Amen.

'Remember this: whoever sows sparingly will also reap sparingly, and whoever sows generously will also reap generously. Each of you should give what you have decided in your heart to give, not reluctantly or under compulsion, for God loves a cheerful giver.'

(2 Corinthians 9 vs 6-8 NIV)

GENTLENESS

Lord God,

We all need to be more gentle and consider more deeply how we speak, treat and behave towards others.

Lord, help us to be politer, kinder and meek in our conversations, attitude and connections with everyone.

Thank you for your goodness to us Lord.

May the words of our mouths and the thoughts of our hearts, bless you name and others, always.

Gently make yourself known to us each day God; heal us, restore us and comfort us.

In Jesus name.

Amen.

• • • • • • •

'Blessed are the meek, for they shall inherit the earth.'
(Matthew 5 vs 5 NLT)

GIVING

Dear Lord,

Help me today to give without remembering and receive without forgetting.

Thank you for giving us your Son Jesus to show us just how much you love us.

Today help me bless someone through giving and to remember to give you our thanks and praise.

Amen.

'It is more blessed to give than to receive.'
(Acts 20 vs 35 NIV)

GOODNESS

Dear God,

Today I thank you for your goodness.

Today I praise you that you are in control.

Today I hand over my worries and concerns and ask for your comfort.

Today may I be a source of goodness for others.

Keep us safe, Lord.

Be near us today and be praised.

Amen.

• • • • • • •

'And God is able to bless you abundantly,
so that in all things at all times, having all that you need,
you will abound in every good work.'

(2 Corinthians 9 vs 8 NIV)

'Trust in the LORD and do good; dwell in the land
and enjoy safe pasture.'

(Psalm 37 vs 3 NIV)

GRACE

Father God,

Thank you, Lord, that your abundant grace is greater than sin in me.

Thank you for your love for us today, Father. Jesus, thank you for giving your life for our sins and overcoming death.

We thank you that we see grace in many things, but the greatest example of all was your Son Jesus coming to die on a cross for each one of us so our sins would be forgiven.

We praise you today and this week for your kindness and compassion to us, and for your grace.

Amen.

'God saved you by his grace when you believed.
And you can't take credit for this; it is a gift from God.
Salvation is not a reward for the good things we have done,
so none of us can boast about it.'

(Ephesians 2 vs 8-9 NLT)

GUIDANCE

Dear Lord,

Guide our lives in your ways of truth and love, kindness and humility.

Help us to receive good advice from others graciously, and use it wisely when we find ourselves at a crossroad or in difficult situations.

Help us to share good counsel with others and advise well.

Help us to learn to trust in you and your word more and more every single day.

Amen.

'Listen to advice and accept instruction,
that you may gain wisdom in the future.'
(Proverbs 19 vs 20 ESV)

HAPPINESS/JOY

Dear Lord,

Help us to seek the values that will bring us lasting joy in this changing world.

We pray for happiness and ask you for joyful, cheerful hearts.

We pray that others are drawn to our happy smiles, our positive attitudes, and faces that shine with joy.

You have created us to be happy, to find joy and laughter in the different stages and experiences of life.

We pray that the cheerful hearts among us lift us and bring joy to everyone around.

Amen.

'May the God of hope fill you with all joy and peace in believing, so that by the power of the Holy Spirit you may abound in hope.'
(Romans 15 vs 13 ESV)

HARVEST/THANKSGIVING

Father God,

We praise you for all that we have, particularly for the harvest and the bountiful food we are able to enjoy in our country.

Thank you for the work of our farmers, for all their sweat, effort and hard work.

We give you thanks for every good thing in our lives.

God, we thank you above everything.

Amen.

'Give thanks in all circumstances; for this is the will of God in Christ Jesus for you.'
(1 Thessalonians 5 vs 18 ESV)

'Giving thanks always and for everything to God the Father in the name of our Lord Jesus Christ.'
(Ephesians 5 vs 20 ESV)

HEALING

Dear Lord,

When we are unwell, restore our bodies to full health.

When we are exhausted, give us your energy to do mighty things.

When we are hurt by unkind words, help us to forgive, like you forgave us.

Thank you for those who work in any form of care work (parents/carers, NHS, care home workers, teachers, police, social workers, etc.). Bless them richly, God.

Help us to heal a hurting world by loving others and doing good.

Amen.

'O Lord my God, I cried to you for help, and you have healed me.'
(Psalm 30 vs 2 ESV)

HEALTH

Dear Lord,

Today I offer you my mind
May I seek the mind of Christ in all things
Freed from anxiety and fear
Filled with health and wholeness
Today I offer you my spirit
In you I have been born again
Your Spirit dwells deeply within me
My Spirit is alive in you
Freed from negative and unhelpful thoughts
Today I offer you my body
May it be a temple dedicated to you, O Lord
A place where you live and reign
May I be mindful of what I eat and drink
May I be careful to take rest and sleep
Lord, right now I offer you my whole being
I present my mind, spirit and body to you
Come and take me as a living sacrifice
This day and everyday
May I ever give you the glory.

Amen.

'The LORD is my strength and my shield; in him my heart trusts, and I am helped; my heart exults, and with my song I give thanks to him.'

(Psalm 28 vs 7 ESV)

HOLY PEOPLE

Dear God,

Thank you for those who are considered to be saints and thank you that you call me a saint, not a sinner.

Help me to learn from the example of holy people and behave in a way that brings light, joy and love to others.

Help me to do all the good I can in this world; to be kind, caring and thoughtful in all I do and say.

May my life be wholly good and pleasing to you. Hear my prayers always that they may be as sweet-smelling incense.

Amen.

'In the same way, the Spirit helps us in our weakness. We do not know what we ought to pray for, but the Spirit himself intercedes for us through wordless groans. And he who searches our hearts knows the mind of the Spirit, because the Spirit intercedes for God's people in accordance with the will of God.'

(Romans 8 vs 26-27 NIV)

HONOUR

Dear Jesus,

One of your commandments says, 'Honour your mother and father.' Help us to appreciate our families, our guardians and our friends, and treat them well.

Help us to do honourable things: showing kindness to all, sharing what we have, going the extra mile for others, and always doing our best at school, and in any other activities we do.

Lastly, let our school be a light in our community, radiating joy and peace towards others.

Amen.

'And whatever you do, in word or deed, do it all in the name of the Lord Jesus, giving thanks to God the Father through him.'

(Colossians 3 vs 17 NIV)

'Worthy are you, our Lord and God, to receive glory and honour and power, for you created all things, and by your will they existed and were created.'

(Revelation 4 vs 11 ESV)

HOPE

Dear God,

Help us to rely on you today and put our trust in Jesus.

Help us to have faith in your promises to us.

Teach us to hold on to hope and believe in a better tomorrow.

Help us us all to dream of a brighter future, for everyone.

Help us to live our lives for you and spread hope in this world, wherever we go.

Thank you for the hope we have in you, Lord.

Amen.

> 'But blessed is the one who trusts in the LORD, whose confidence is in him. They will be like a tree planted by the water that sends out its roots by the stream. It does not fear when heat comes; its leaves are always green. It has no worries in a year of drought and never fails to bear fruit.'
>
> (Jeremiah 17:7-8 NIV)

HUMILITY

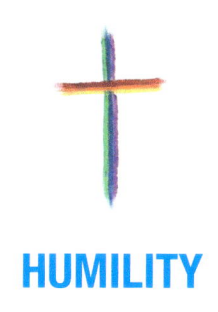

Dear God,

Teach me to be humble this day, to show humility.

I put my trust in you for all things.

I rely on you for wisdom.

I seek understanding from your word and want to be more like you.

Holy Spirit, help me to learn and show Jesus' characteristics in my life.

Help me to be humble before I am proud; thankful before I boast.

Amen.

'If my people, who are called by my name, will humble themselves and pray and seek my face and turn from their wicked ways, then I will hear from heaven, and I will forgive their sin and will heal their land.'

(2 Chronicles 7 vs 14 NIV)

INDIVIDUALITY

Dear Lord,

Thank you that each one of us is different, we are all unique and special.

Thank you that we can express who we are through our individuality, the way we share with the world what we think, how we feel and who we are.

Help us to be thankful for every blessing we have and remember to express ourselves through our individuality, tactfully and respectful of others.

As we learn and discover who we are, help us to discover more about you too, God.

Amen.

'For the body does not consist of one member but of many. If the foot should say, "Because I am not a hand, I do not belong to the body", that would not make it any less a part of the body. And if the ear should say, "Because I am not an eye, I do not belong to the body", that would not make it any less a part of the body. If the whole body were an eye, where would be the sense of hearing? If the whole body were an ear, where would be the sense of smell? But as it is, God arranged the members in the body, each one of them, as he chose. If all were a single member, where would the body be? As it is, there are many parts, yet one body.'

(1 Corinthians 12 vs 14-20 ESV)

INFLUENCE

Dear Lord,

It is so easy to be influenced by others, to do good or bad things.

Help me to be influenced by the right things and the right people who have good hearts and sound judgement.

Help me to positively influence others when they might not be doing the right thing or making the right decisions.

God, help me to manage peer pressure, and always do what is right, even when it's not the 'easy' thing to do.

Amen.

'Give instruction to a wise man, and he will be still wiser; teach a righteous man, and he will increase in learning.'
(Proverbs 9 vs 9 ESV)

INNER HEALING

Dear Lord,

When things seem unfair and the words of others are unkind, give us the strength of an inner calm and gentleness of spirit.

Help us to respond to others with gentleness and kindness. Heal our hearts and minds Lord, by your Spirit.

And, where there is hurt, let me bring forgiveness and where there in injury, the gentle balm of healing.

Help me to give my neighbour compassion and understanding, to treat them with the kindness I would like to receive, when I get things wrong.

Peace be with us all this day.

Amen

'Take my yoke upon you, and learn from me, for I am gentle and lowly in heart, and you will find rest for your souls'.
(Matthew 11 vs 12 ESV)

INTELLIGENCE

Dear God,

Help us to learn at school so that we can grow in maturity, become more informed and make wise decisions, daily.

Help us to be thankful for our teachers and for anyone in our lives who teaches us what is right and wrong.

As we focus on acquiring knowledge, skills and wisdom during our time at school, prepare us, Lord, for the wider world in which we live.

Amen.

• • • • • • •

'Having gifts that differ according to the grace given to us, let us use them: if prophecy, in proportion to our faith; if service, in our serving; the one who teaches, in his teaching; the one who exhorts, in his exhortation; the one who contributes, in generosity; the one who leads, with zeal; the one who does acts of mercy, with cheerfulness.'

(Romans 12 vs 6-8 ESV)

JESUS, THE FIRST AND THE LAST!

Dear Jesus,

Lord of my heart, my only God.

Be my waking thought, my breath this day.

Be by my side, whatever this day brings.

Guide me, lift my spirits and make yourself known to me.

And Lord, when I close my eyes again tonight, watch over me as I sleep.

Amen.

'For God so loved the world, that he gave his only Son, that whoever believes in him should not perish but have eternal life.'

(John 3 vs 16 ESV)

'He is the radiance of the glory of God and the exact imprint of his nature, and he upholds the universe by the word of his power. After making purification for sins, he sat down at the right hand of the Majesty on high.'

(Hebrews 1 vs 3 ESV)

JOURNEYS

Dear Lord Jesus,

Thank you for the journey we have been on and the special memories we have created this past academic year. Help us to remember what we have learned and put it to good use in the future.

Thank you for this year, for the community we have been a part of and for the achievements of all. As we continue striving for progress and success, help us to use this year as a platform for greater things in the next phase of our school journey.

Thank you for all the hard-working staff, parents and carers and all the people who have helped us on our way. Help us to use times of rest and refreshment wisely, to recuperate, reflect and dream.

As we journey through life Holy Spirit, continue to guide us always.

Amen.

'"For I know the plans I have for you," declares the Lord, "plans to prosper you and not to harm you, plans to give you hope and a future."'
(Jeremiah 29 vs 11 NIV)

JOY

Dear God,

Help us to see, hear and feel joy this day.

Help me to bring joy to others too.

Pick us up, Lord, when we are feeling low.

Comfort those who need you now.

Walk beside us today, God, and be near.

Thank you!

Amen.

'May the God of hope fill you with all joy and peace as you trust in him, so that you may overflow with hope by the power of the Holy Spirit.'

(Romans 15 vs 13 NIV)

'Love. Joy. Peace. Patience. Kindness. Goodness. Faithfulness. Gentleness, and Self-control. To these, I commit my day.'

(Anonymous)

JUSTICE

Dear God,

You are the God of justice, quick to forgive and mighty to save.

Please guide our school into the way of justice and truth, and give us your peace.

Help us to forgive others when they have wronged us, and restore, heal and rebuild damaged friendships.

Let justice prevail in all the terrible situations in the world, and let the hope of so many poor, war-ravaged, downtrodden and lonely people be heard.

Help us to always do the right thing, and be thankful for what good things we have.

Amen.

• • • • • • •

'Justice, and only justice, you shall follow, that you may live and inherit the land that the LORD your God is giving you.'

(Deuteronomy 16 vs 20 ESV)

'Righteousness and justice are the foundation of your throne; steadfast love and faithfulness go before you.'

(Psalm 89 vs 14 ESV)

KINDNESS

Dear Lord,

Each and every day I have an opportunity to be kind. Help me make those life-changing choices and make others smile.

Thank you for all the kindness shown by the adults at our school, for the extra mile the staff go to help us succeed in becoming a better person or achieving our full potential.

Help me to speak a kind word or do a kind deed and expect nothing in return.

We pray for all those in need of kindness today. Prompt me to do something for them and make a difference in this world.

Help us all be more selfless and to put others first throughout this day and beyond.

Amen.

● ● ● ● ● ● ●

'May the LORD now show you kindness and faithfulness, and I too will show you the same favour because you have done this.'

(2 Samuel 2 vs 6 NIV)

'Kind hearts are the garden,
Kind thoughts are the roots,
Kind words are the flowers,
Kind deeds are the fruits.'

(John Ruskin)

KOINONIA

Christian fellowship or communion with God or with fellow Christians; said in particular of the early Christian community.

Dear Lord,

Let us join together with you in prayer for a happy, uplifting and successful year.

Help us to grow as people and showcase our best talents.

Helps us to be the best we can be every single day, in our lessons, outside of school and at home.

Help us to be polite, kind and caring individuals. Make us thankful for all the staff in this school and for all they do for us.

As a community, help us to grow together, learn together and be successful.

Amen.

• • • • • • • •

'They devoted themselves to the apostles' teaching and to fellowship, to the breaking of bread and to prayer. Everyone was filled with awe at the many wonders and signs performed by the apostles. All the believers were together and had everything in common. They sold property and possessions to give to anyone who had need. Every day they continued to meet together in the temple courts. They broke bread in their homes and ate together with glad and sincere hearts, praising God and enjoying the favour of all the people. And the Lord added to their number daily those who were being saved.'

(Acts 2 vs 42-47 NIV)

LEADERSHIP

Lord,

We ask, we need and we pray for wisdom during uncertain times.

Give our leaders wisdom to make the right decisions for us all.

As we read your Word, God, teach us new things.

Help us to make wise choices and do our best at this time.

Help us to respect, obey and support our leaders too, and recognise the difficult decisions they have to make.

We pray for you to be at the centre of our school, Jesus.

Amen.

'Do not forsake wisdom, and she will protect you; love her, and she will watch over you. The beginning of wisdom is this: get wisdom. Though it cost all you have, get understanding.'

(Proverbs 4 vs 6-7 NIV)

LEARNING

Lord God,

Today we thank you for the opportunity that learning brings us throughout our whole lives.

For the ability to learn and be taught, we thank you.

Bless the educators in school and at home, our teachers, parents, family members, carers and friends.

Help us to learn truth from your Word, learn how to live as we are born to live and bring you glory.

Thank you for learning today – the plain old learning and the all-inspiring WOW learning!

Amen.

• • • • • • • •

'I will instruct you and teach you in the way you should go;
I will counsel you with my loving eye on you.'

(Psalm 32 vs 8 NIV)

'Let the message of Christ dwell among you richly as you teach and admonish one another with all wisdom through psalms, hymns, and songs from the Spirit, singing to God with gratitude in your hearts.'

(Colossians 3 vs 16 NIV)

LEISURE

Dear God,

During this week of hard work and assessment, help us to take time out and relax.

Remind us that we need to have a healthy balance in our lives between work, play and rest.

Help us to use our free time wisely, to recuperate, revitalise and refresh ourselves.

Thank you that when we have the right balance, we can give our absolute best in all things.

Be with all of us this week as we focus and do our very best.

Help us to make the school and ourselves proud.

Amen.

'He makes me lie down in green pastures; he leads me beside quiet waters.'
(Psalm 23 vs 2 NIV)

LENT / EASTER

Dear God,

Thank you for this special time of year when we particularly remember what Jesus did for each one of us on the cross.

Help us to remember that this was only half of the story; that he rose again and is with us every day through the Holy Spirit.

Thank you for this, God, that you love us all so much you allowed your Son to come to earth to die, that we might have life. What a miracle, what a good God you are, compassionate and loving.

Help each one of us to remember this special season, one of newness and life. Give us a new energy to do what is right, good and praiseworthy in your sight.

Let us remember what Lent has taught us about sacrifice and perseverance and let us use the story of Easter and the events of Holy Week to understand that you want us to live life in its fullness, knowing you.

Thank you for Jesus, for your Holy Spirit and for loving each one of us, God.

Amen.

'For God so loved the world that he gave his one and only Son, that whoever believes in him shall not perish but have eternal life.'

(John 3 vs 16 NIV)

LIGHT

God the Trinity can be described like light:
the source = Father God
the light = Jesus
the heat = Holy Spirit

Dear Lord God,

Thank you that you are the light of the world, enabling us to see truth from lies, right from wrong.

Thank you for your example of showing us how to behave.

Help us to be more like you: a light to those around us, warm and friendly, caring and respectful.

God, reveal to us our faults, and guide us when we lose direction in life. Help us to seek you in times of trouble.

Finally, God, thank you that even the smallest light can overcome the very darkest of darkness. Let us remember this, and let it give us hope!

Amen.

'Let your light shine before others, so that they may see your good works and give glory to your Father who is in heaven.'
(Matthew 5 vs 16 ESV)

LIGHT

Father God,

Bring light into my life this day; beautiful people, music, birdsong, nature, a smell, a card in the post, or something else special.

Help me to be a light for others; to guide, to help, and to brighten their day.

For your glory today, help me to bring joy to this world.

Amen.

'A saint is someone the light shines through.'
(Anonymous)

LIMITS

Dear Lord God,

With you there are no limits and nothing is impossible.

Thank you that we have hope in a God who is unrivalled.

Today and tomorrow, help us to go beyond limits of what is expected of us and be better than we were yesterday.

Help us to do better in a world where who we are, our race, religion and gender do not get in the way of our progress.

Be with us as we step into a world of limitless opportunities; help us to do what is good.

Thank you that you can do all things!

Amen.

'For nothing will be impossible with God.'
(Luke 1 vs 37 ESV)

LISTENING

Father God,

Speak to me when I focus on you and help me to be a good listener today.

Remind me to put others first and truly listen to them.

Thank you for our friends and family whom we love greatly and who are always ready to listen to us.

Thank you that when we are alone, you are there ready, waiting to listen to us too.

In the quiet times today, help me to listen to you.

Thank you, Lord.

Amen.

'In the morning, Lord, you hear my voice; in the morning I lay my requests before you and wait expectantly.'

(Psalm 5 vs 3 NIV)

LOSS

Lord God,

You know what it is like to lose someone you love, whether that is a person or a beloved pet.

Please help anyone experiencing loss at this time who is consumed with overwhelming grief.

Turn their eyes to you as they seek to find strength and comfort.

Show your compassion, Lord. Help those who need your help through their pain and help us to be a support to anyone we know who is grieving.

Amen.

• • • • • • •

'When the righteous cry for help, the Lord hears and delivers them out of all their troubles. The Lord is near to the broken-hearted and saves the crushed in spirit. Many are the afflictions of the righteous, but the Lord delivers him out of them all. He keeps all his bones; not one of them is broken.'

(Psalm 34 vs 17-20 ESV)

'Blessed are those who mourn, for they shall be comforted.'

(Matthew 5 vs 4 ESV)

LOVE

Dear Lord,

Thank you that you love each and every one of us enough to have died on a cross for us.

Thank you that you want each of us to know your love, every single day of our lives.

Help us this day to cherish and be thankful for our loved ones. Bless each of our family members and friends, God.

We pray for those who have lost loved ones up and down this country, and across the world. Comfort them all.

Help us this day love our neighbours as we do ourselves, to love our enemies and love you with all our hearts.

Thank you for always loving us and for showing us what true love looks like, God.

Help us to feel your love in our hearts today.

Amen.

'God proved his love on the cross. When Christ hung, and bled, and died, it was God saying to the world, "I love you."'

(Billy Graham)

'A new commandment I give to you, that you love one another: just as I have loved you, you also are to love one another. By this all people will know that you are my disciples, if you have love for one another.'

(John 13 vs 34-35 ESV)

LOYALTY

Dear Lord,

Thank you for the quality of loyalty and support.

Teach us to use this quality in life and be loyal to our family and friends, our workplace and in all that we do.

Thank you for your faithfulness, Lord, and your desire to know each one of us more.

Help us to want to know you more too.

Amen.

'Let not steadfast love and faithfulness forsake you; bind them around your neck; write them on the tablet of your heart. So you will find favour and good success in the sight of God and man. Trust in the Lord with all your heart, and do not lean on your own understanding. In all your ways acknowledge him, and he will make straight your paths. Be not wise in your own eyes; fear the Lord, and turn away from evil. It will be healing to your flesh and refreshment to your bones.'

(Proverbs 3 vs 3-8 ESV)

MANNERS

Dear God,

Help us to learn at school so that we can grow, mature and make wise decisions each day.

Help us to be thankful for our teachers and for anyone in our lives who teaches us what is right and wrong.

As we focus on acquiring knowledge, skills and wisdom during our time at school, prepare us for the wider world in which we live.

In Jesus' name we pray.

Amen.

'For the LORD grants wisdom! From his mouth come knowledge and understanding. He grants a treasure of common sense to the honest. He is a shield to those who walk with integrity.'

(Proverbs 2 vs 6-7 NLT)

ME

Dear Lord Jesus,

Remind us to value our individuality and celebrate differences.

Help us to remember we are made in your image, beautiful and wonderfully made.

Holy Spirit, help us to become more like Jesus in words and deeds.

May we all use our gifts, talents and hearts to do good, and to bring you praise.

Help me to remember how special I am to you, perfect in your sight.

Amen.

'For you formed my inward parts; you knitted me together in my mother's womb. I praise you, for I am fearfully and wonderfully made. Wonderful are your works; my soul knows it very well. My frame was not hidden from you, when I was being made in secret, intricately woven in the depths of the earth. Your eyes saw my unformed substance; in your book were written, every one of them, the days that were formed for me, when as yet there was none of them.'

(Psalm 139 vs 13-16 ESV)

MORNING

Jesus, Lord of my heart, my God.

Be my waking thought, my breath this day.

Thank you for the morning, a new start with you, God.

Be there by my side, whatever this day brings.

Help me to appreciate this new day and praise you for it.

Thank you!

Amen.

'In the morning, LORD, you hear my voice;
in the morning I lay my requests before you and wait expectantly.'
(Psalm 5 vs 3 NIV)

MOTIVATION

Dear God,

When I start to lose motivation, give me the strength to work hard.

When I feel unmotivated and tired, give me the energy to do something good.

When I face difficult moments and make wrong turns, guide me, Lord.

When I fail to behave as I should, help me to mend my ways and be sorry.

Refresh my spirit, refresh my body, refresh my soul this day.

Thank you!

Amen.

• • • • • • •

'But they who wait for the LORD shall renew their strength; they shall mount up with wings like eagles; they shall run and not be weary; they shall walk and not faint.'

(Isaiah 40 vs 31 ESV)

MOVING ON (to a new school)/ DREAMS (following our)

Dear Lord Jesus,

Help us to remember our time at school with teachers and friends and the special memories we have created this past year.

Help us to use what we have learned, in and out of lessons, to put this to good use in the future.

Thank you for this year, for the community we have been a part of here at school and for the achievements of all.

We are so fortunate to be part of such a wonderful community, so help us to use this year as a platform for greater things in the next phase of our school journey.

Thank you for all the hard-working staff, the parents and all the people who have helped us on our way.

May our summer break be a time of rest and refreshing, a time to reflect and dream. Please help to guide and inspire us, Lord.

In Jesus' name.

Amen.

'Do not be anxious about anything, but in everything by prayer and supplication with thanksgiving let your requests be made known to God.'
(Philippians 4 vs 6 ESV)

MUSIC

Lord Jesus,

Thank you for the richness, the beauty and the wonder of music.

Thank you that music is an antidote to many of life's stresses.

When we hear instruments play, or voices sing, we praise you for that talent.

When we sing, be praised, for it is our worship to you.

We thank you that music speaks to us, that it can give us a voice and it can even be our prayer to you.

Help us to make more music in this world and share it to bring you and others joy, God.

Amen.

'What am I to do? I will pray with my spirit, but I will pray with my mind also; I will sing praise with my spirit, but I will sing with my mind also.'

(1 Corinthians 14 vs 15 ESV)

NEW TERM

Lord God,

At the beginning of this new term teach us to be your hands and feet.

At the beginning of this new term teach us to love others as you love us.

At the beginning of this new term teach us to pray for those in need.

Help us to work hard, do our best and show kindness and compassion to all.

Amen.

'We can make our plans, but the Lord determines our steps.'
(Proverbs 16 vs 9 NLT)

OPPORTUNITIES

Dear Lord Jesus,

Thank you for the opportunity that play and recreation bring; the enjoyment, the learning, and a rest from hard work.

It is wonderful that our school has so much on offer at break and lunch times, and throughout the day. Make us thankful, Lord – how blessed we are!

Help us, with our parents' and carers' permission, to make the most of the opportunities we are given at home, at school and in our community.

Help us to try different activities, learn and develop new skills, so that we may make new friends and discover more about ourselves.

Finally, we thank you for all the staff and those people who enable us to take part in these activities, who give up their time, support and teach us.

In Jesus' name.

Amen.

• • • • • • •

'So then, as we have opportunity, let us do good to everyone, and especially to those who are of the household of faith.'

(Galatians 6 vs 10 ESV)

PARTNERSHIP

Dear Lord,

Thank you that by working together in partnership, so much more can be achieved.

We praise you that co-operation and teamwork are essential to society and life, and we get to practise so much here at school.

Teach us to use our skills for the good of others, share bright ideas to further our learning and together make this world a better place for all.

Amen.

• • • • • • • •

'Two are better than one, because they have a good reward for their toil.'
(Ecclesiastes 4 vs 9 ESV)

PATIENCE

Dear God,

We pray today for patience.

Give us patience with one another when emotions run high and when we get frustrated.

Help us to find a moment in the day to be still, to stop for a few minutes and pause for thought.

Help us to reflect on what is most important and be mindful of others' needs before our own.

Let us focus on what is good and just and right today, being quick to forgive and to say sorry.

Help us to be patient with each other today.

Amen.

• • • • • • •

'May you be strengthened with all power, according to his glorious might, for all endurance and patience with joy.'
(Colossians 1 vs 11 ESV)

PEACE

Dear God,

We give you praise for your abundant mercy and grace that we daily receive.

We thank you for your faithfulness.

Lord Jesus, we ask you to give us peace of mind, body, soul and spirit today.

Heal and remove everything that causes stress, grief and sorrow in our lives.

Please guide our path and help us to find peace and quiet in the busyness of life.

Let your peace reign in our families, in our school and everything we do.

In Jesus' name

Amen.

• • • • • • •

'Peace I leave with you; my peace I give to you. Not as the world gives do I give to you. Let not your hearts be troubled, neither let them be afraid.'
(John 14 vs 27 ESV)

PEACE (inner)

Almighty God,

We bless you for our lives. We give you praise for the abundant mercy and grace we receive from you.

We thank you for your faithfulness even though we are often not that faithful to you.

Lord Jesus, we ask you to give us peace in our mind, body, soul and spirit.

We want you to heal and remove everything that is causing stress, grief, and sorrow in our lives.

We also ask for peace in this war torn and troubled world.

Amen.

• • • • • • •

'Peace I leave with you; my peace I give you. I do not give as the world gives. Do not let your hearts be troubled and do not be afraid.'

(John 14 vs 27 NIV)

PERSEVERANCE

Dear Lord,

Help me to be courageous in my work, to take risks and dare to make mistakes.

Give me courage when life is tough, when I'm feeling down and I feel like giving up.

Please give me the courage, Lord, to confront my fears, and the strength to carry on when a situation is difficult or when I feel like giving up.

Help me do what is right, stand against any form of wrongdoing and persevere to do all the good I can on earth.

Amen.

'Be strong, and let your heart take courage, all you who wait for the Lord!'
(Psalm 31 vs 24 ESV)

PERSONALITY

Dear God,

Thank you for kind friends and for smiley teachers. Also, thank you for our pets that we love.

We are grateful that each of us has a personality, unique and individual, that makes us who we are.

Help us to appreciate the variety of personalities we have in our school, and the mix of characters. This is what makes our school special and interesting, and why meeting new people and making new friends is fun!

Help us to develop our good nature, the caring side to our being where kindness rules.

Lord, help us be our best and shine!

Amen.

'Put on your new nature, created to be like God – truly righteous and holy.'
(Ephesians 4 vs 24 NLT)

PHYSICAL HEALTH

Dear Lord,

Help us to take care of our bodies by eating well, exercising and resting.

We pray for those who are currently unwell, whether it be family members or friends. God, heal any problem they might have so that they can return to full health.

Remind us that cleanliness and self-respect are important to maintaining good physical health.

Thank you that each one of us is unique and wonderfully made and loved by you.

Amen.

'Do you not know that your body is a temple of the Holy Spirit within you, whom you have from God? You are not your own, for you were bought with a price. So glorify God in your body.'

(1 Corinthians 6 vs 19-20 ESV)

PLAY

Lord God,

Thank you that you want us to have fun and play.

Thank you that we all have different interests and love of activities.

Be with us, Lord, in the good times; enjoy seeing your people being happy and hopefully making others happy too.

Remind us that play brings balance to our lives and helps restore us.

Give us today opportunities to play.

Amen.

'And the streets of the city shall be full of boys and girls playing in its streets.'
(Zechariah 8 vs 5 ESV)

PLEASURE

Dear Lord,

Thank you that we are able to seek pleasure in many things, particularly our hobbies and the things we love in life.

Remind us, Lord, how fortunate we are to be able to have freedom to enjoy these things, and we think of those who find little pleasure in their lives.

Help us all to find pleasure in being generous, in doing good towards others and through the kind words we speak.

Help us to be careful to find pleasure in the right things, and stay away from all kinds of wrongdoing.

In Jesus' name.

Amen.

'So flee youthful passions and pursue righteousness, faith, love, and peace, along with those who call on the Lord from a pure heart.'

(2 Timothy 2 vs 22 ESV)

'Doing wrong is fun for a fool, but living wisely brings pleasure to the sensible.'

(Proverbs 10 vs 23 NLT)

PRAYER

Dear God,

Thank you that today you hear our prayers – you hear the prayers of all your people.

We can come to you in prayer to praise you, ask your forgiveness, ask for a favour and show gratitude.

As we speak to you, hear our heartfelt prayer requests.

Lord, let your will be done today.

Thank you!

Amen.

'In the morning, Lord, you hear my voice; in the morning I lay my requests before you and wait expectantly.'

(Psalm 5 vs 3 NIV)

PRIORITIES

Dear Lord,

Help us to focus on the important things in life: you in all your holiness, our family, friends, our (school) work and maintaining healthy bodies and minds. Help us to put these first in our lives.

So many things can get in the way of what is important, what is priority. Help us to see clearly what a priority is and what is not.

Lord, please help us to remember time for quiet, for prayer, contemplation and reflection. We thank you that you draw close to us when we are down and rejoice with us when we are happy.

In Jesus' name.

Amen.

'For where your treasure is, there your heart will be also.'
(Luke 12 vs 34 NIV)

'And he said to his disciples, "Therefore I tell you, do not be anxious about your life, what you will eat, nor about your body, what you will put on. For life is more than food, and the body more than clothing. Consider the ravens: they neither sow nor reap, they have neither storehouse nor barn, and yet God feeds them. Of how much more value are you than the birds! And which of you by being anxious can add a single hour to his span of life? If then you are not able to do as small a thing as that, why are you anxious about the rest?'
(Luke 12 vs 22-26 ESV)

PROTECTION

Lord God,

I ask for your protection this day for my family and friends.

Be at my side and be my refuge.

Protect those working at the heart of this global pandemic.

Thank you for those who care for and serve others.

Be a shield for the vulnerable, Lord, and be a comfort to those in fear.

Surround us all with your unending love, God, and protect us this day.

Amen.

'He who dwells in the shelter of the Most High will abide in the shadow of the Almighty. I will say to the LORD, "My refuge and my fortress, my God, in whom I trust" . . . "Because he holds fast to me in love, I will deliver him; I will protect him because he knows my name."

(Psalm 91 vs 1-2, 14 ESV)

PUNCTUALITY

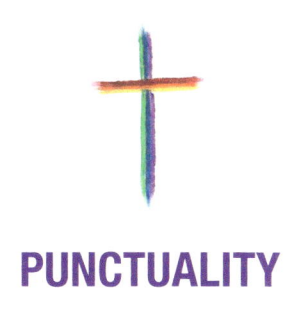

Dear God,

Help us to show that we care about our education by being on time to school.

Thank you that your timing is perfect and you have always set a perfect example.

Help us to plan our homework and manage our time effectively, so that we meet deadlines.

Let us prioritise work, rest and play and always think of others first.

Help us to show respect to others by turning up on time when expected, but be quick to forgive when others are late through no fault of their own.

Amen.

'Each of you look not only to his own interests,
but also to the interests of others.'
(Philippians 2 vs 4 ESV)

READINESS

Dear Lord God,

Help us to be prepared for whatever life brings.

Remind us to be punctual, have the right equipment and be ready to learn

If we aren't feeling our best, help us to manage our emotions and just do our best.

Thank you to our teachers who prepare so much for us in advance.

Amen.

'Remind the believers to submit to the government and its officers. They should be obedient, always ready to do what is good.'

(Titus 3 vs 1 NLT)

'Those too lazy to plough in the right season will have no food at the harvest.'

(Proverbs 20 vs 4 NLT)

RECIPROCITY

Dear Lord God,

Thank you for the many examples in the Bible of teamwork and collaboration: Adam and Eve, Moses and Aaron, Jesus and his disciples to name a few.

Help us to realise the importance of working together, supporting each other and accepting advice when we most need it. Remind us that we are never alone, for you are always with us.

At school, please help us to do our best in all lessons, to help others learn by supporting them, and by not disrupting the learning of others.

Help us to become more resilient, prepared to lead our own learning or be led and work with others in order to get work done.

We thank you, Lord.

Amen.

'And Jesus said to them, "Follow me, and I will make you become fishers of men."'
(Mark 1 vs 17 ESV)

RECOGNITION

Dear Lord,

Help me to recognise all that you do for me.

Help me to recognise what others do for me: family, friends and teachers, and be grateful to them all.

Help me to say thank you when it is deserved and right to do so.

Make me thankful, Lord.

Amen.

'Finally, brothers, whatever is true, whatever is honourable, whatever is just, whatever is pure, whatever is lovely, whatever is commendable, if there is any excellence, if there is anything worthy of praise, think about these things. What you have learned and received and heard and seen in me – practise these things, and the God of peace will be with you.'

(Philippians 4 vs 8-10 ESV)

REFLECTION

Lord,

Help me to reflect on my life, its good points and bad.

Teach me how I can become a better person in my words, thoughts and deeds, just like Jesus.

When I read your word in the Bible, speak to me.

Give me the strength to recognise where I can improve and be better.

Help me to treat others in this world with kindness and love my enemy.

Amen.

'Do not be conformed to this world, but be transformed by the renewal of your mind, that by testing you may discern what is the will of God, what is good and acceptable and perfect.'

(Romans 12 vs 2 ESV)

REFLECTIVENESS

Dear Lord,

Help us to reflect on what is right and what is good.

Help us to evaluate our lives, and work to improve areas for development.

Help us to become better planners, planning work more carefully.

Help us to be willing to revise, monitor and change what we do.

Help us to reflect on you, and on all the blessings you give us.

Help us to acknowledge difficulties and be strong enough to overcome them.

Amen.

'And we all, with unveiled face, beholding the glory of the Lord, are being transformed into the same image from one degree of glory to another. For this comes from the Lord who is the Spirit.'

(2 Corinthians 3 vs 18 ESV)

REJOICE

Lord God,

Let me look to the heavens and sing your praises.

Let me look at my riches and thank you for them.

Help me to realise my worth to you, and sing in my heart.

Help me to share your good news with others.

Today, I praise you here on earth.

May the words of my mouth and the thoughts of my heart bless your name!

Amen.

'May the words of my mouth and the meditation of my heart be pleasing to you, O LORD, my rock and my redeemer.'

(Psalm 19 vs 14 NLT)

RELATIONSHIPS

Dear Lord Jesus,

Relationships are fundamental to life, so important, and no relationship is more important than having a relationship with you.

Help us to cherish the relationships we have with family, friends and people we know. Help us to be kind to all we meet, and, Lord, help us to build strong, lasting friendships through mutual trust and kindness, respect, care and love.

When we face difficulties in our relationships, God, give us all strength, patience and grace.

Finally, may a love for others shine through each one of us just like your love for us. Help us to work on and improve our relationships this week through good actions and kind words.

In Jesus' name.

Amen.

'And above all these put on love, which binds everything together in perfect harmony.'

(Colossians 3 vs 14 ESV)

'And let us consider how we may spur one another on towards love and good deeds, not giving up meeting together, as some are in the habit of doing, but encouraging one another.'

(Hebrew 10 vs 24-25 NIV)

RELIABILITY

Dear Father,

Thank you for Jesus who came to serve us on earth and who gave his life for us.

Show us how we can be a help in our communities, how we can serve our family and friends and put others first.

Humble us, Lord, so that we give gladly, obediently and faithfully, without looking for praise or thanks.

Help us to show the quality of reliability in our lives, so others might be able to trust and depend on us in times of need.

Amen.

'Whatever you do, work heartily, as for the Lord and not for men, knowing that from the Lord you will receive the inheritance as your reward. You are serving the Lord Christ.'

(Colossians 3 vs 23-24 ESV)

REMEMBRANCE

Dear Father God,

We remember today all those who selflessly sacrificed their lives for our freedom, in World War 1. We honour them in our prayers, and we lift their lives up to you. We pray for their families too.

We thank you for every individual who served their country, those who perished, and those who were left with the horrendous memories of such an awful war.

We do not forget what our veterans did for us, or what our armed forces do for us on a daily basis, all around the world. Lord, guide their values, their hearts and give them wisdom.

God, we thank you for those who protect us from evil.
Bless those who vie for peace, justice, honour and goodness.
Help us to follow in their footsteps throughout our lives.

Thank you for Jesus, an innocent man who did no wrong, who was sacrificed on a cross for all our sins.

Finally, help us to learn from past mistakes, be thankful for each day and work towards a more peaceful and prosperous future for all.

Amen.

'Blessed are the poor in spirit, for theirs is the kingdom of heaven.
Blessed are those who mourn, for they shall be comforted.
Blessed are the meek, for they shall inherit the earth.'

(Matthew 5 vs 3-5 NIV)

RENEWAL

Father God,

Help all of us to change for the better at this school, so that we might be a shining light for all to see

May our values, kindness, dedication to hard work, respect for others and care in the community be a beacon of light for you.

Renew in us today a hope in Jesus, a belief that we can be world changers, and the perseverance to strive to achieve our dreams.

Bless our school; all the staff, all the pupils, all the parents, carers and guardians who support us.

Amen.

'He saved us, not because of righteous things we had done, but because of his mercy. He saved us through the washing of rebirth and renewal by the Holy Spirit, whom he poured out on us generously through Jesus Christ our Saviour.'

(Titus 3 vs 5-6 NIV)

REPAIR

Dear Lord,

When we are weak, low, broken or damaged, you restore us and repair the hurt and pain inside. Thank you, Lord.

Help each one of us to make a difference in a world where many people face extremely sad and difficult situations in all parts of this earth

Help us to help the hungry, the homeless and the lonely in whichever ways we can.

Help us to repair broken friendships and make things right where they are not.

Amen.

'And the God of all grace, who called you to his eternal glory in Christ, after you have suffered a little while, will himself restore you and make you strong, firm and steadfast.'

(Peter 5 vs 10 NIV)

RESOURCEFULNESS

Dear Lord God,

Help us in this wasteful world to be more resourceful and respect all that we have and all that we are given.

Make us aware of our personal strengths, and help us to make the best of all situations.

Help us to be resourceful in our learning, using our time, talent, energy and our minds wisely.

Help us to take more responsibility for our own progress and learning, and become more resilient to setbacks.

Teach us, Lord, to see value in objects and ideas, but most of all in people.

And finally, remind us to repair, reduce, reuse, and recycle.

Amen.

'And when they had eaten their fill, he told his disciples, "Gather up the leftover fragments, that nothing may be lost."'
(John 6 vs 12 ESV)

RESPECT

Father God,

Today remind us to respect each other.

Remind us to consider others' feelings, wishes and rights.

We thank you that we are each made in your image, grateful for the abilities and qualities you give to each one of us.

Help us to celebrate all people and their achievements.

We respect you this day, God, and give it to you.

Amen.

> 'Do nothing out of selfish ambition or vain conceit. Rather, in humility value others above yourselves.'
>
> (Philippians 2 vs 3 NIV)

RESPONSIBILITIES

Dear Almighty God,

Lord of all creation, we pray from our weary and groaning world at breaking point and on the verge of unforeseen consequences.

Remind of us of our responsibilities as stewards on this planet, to care for life and have dominion over it.

Help us to place the needs of our planet, animals and others before ourselves.

Amen.

'For each one will bear his own load.'
(Galatians 6 vs 5 ESV)

REVERENCE

Dear Lord,

You are an awesome God; kind, tender-hearted, and merciful.

You love us with an everlasting love; you are always concerned for us.

Thank you that you are all that we need; help us to remember that you are there for us.

Today, receive our respect.

We bless you, Lord, and give you thanks. We lift up our praises to you, God, our Father.

Amen.

'Let all the earth fear the LORD;
let all the inhabitants of the world stand in awe of him!
For he spoke, and it came to be; he commanded,
and it stood firm.'
(Psalm 33 vs 8-9 ESV)

RIGHT AND WRONG

Dear God,

You are the God of justice, quick to forgive and mighty to save.

Please guide our school into the way of justice and truth, and give us your peace today.

Help us to forgive others when they have wronged us, and restore, heal and rebuild damaged friendships.

Let justice prevail in all the terrible situations in the world, and let the hope of so many poor, war-ravaged, downtrodden and lonely people be heard.

Help each one of us to do things right, and be thankful for what good things we have.

Amen.

'He has told you, O man, what is good; and what does the Lord require of you but to do justice, and to love kindness, and to walk humbly with your God?'

(Micah 6 vs 8 ESV)

RISK-TAKING

Dear Lord,

Give us courage to take 'sensible' risks, which might improve our learning.

Help us to be brave to try new things, and to stretch ourselves.

Remind us that when we fail, we can learn from such failures and do better next time.

Help us to invest our talents wisely without fear, and to use them for good.

Help us to learn, love, shine, to become more resilient as learners, as we face life's problems.

Lord, thank you for taking a risk with us; without it there would be no life at all!

Amen.

'For God gave us a spirit not of fear but of power and love and self-control.'
(2 Timothy 1 vs 7 ESV)

SACRIFICE

Lord God,

Help us to share what we have with others: our time, our advice, our belongings, and kindness.

Thank you that you shared yourself with us and taught us how to live.

Help us to share your good news and our best attributes with everyone.

When joy comes from sharing, may we pass that on to others, Lord.

Thank you that you bless those who are generous in spirit and those who love.

Thank you for your sacrifice for us on a cross, an act of true love.

Thank you, Jesus.

Amen.

'And do not forget to do good and to share with others, for with such sacrifices God is pleased.'

(Hebrews 13 vs 16 NIV)

SAFETY (Community)

Dear Lord,

Thank you for all those in our community who help us to be safe, who have our safety at heart.

You are a God who holds us in the palm of his hand and wants what is good for us.

Help us to be safe, Lord, and help us to think about our actions and the consequences that follow.

Let us make our own safety and that of others our priority in order that everything runs smoothly.

Thank you, God, that your name is a strong tower, somewhere for us to turn in times of trouble.

We ask these things in Jesus' name.

Amen.

'If you make the LORD your refuge, if you make the Most High your shelter, no evil will conquer you; no plague will come near your home.'

(Psalm 91:9-10 NLT)

SAFETY (School)

Dear Lord,

Thank you for all the people in our school who keep us safe, who have our safety at heart.

You are a God who has his people at the forefront of his mind, and you want what is good for us all.

Help us to be safe, Lord, and help us to think about our actions and the consequences that follow.

Let us make our own safety and that of others our priority in order for everything to run smoothly.

Thank you, God, that your name is a strong tower, somewhere for us to turn in times of trouble.

Amen.

'Because you have made the Lord your dwelling place – the Most High, who is my refuge – no evil shall be allowed to befall you.'
(Psalm 91 vs 9-10 ESV)

SAINTS

Dear God,

Thank you for those who are considered to be saints and thank you that you call me a saint, not a sinner

Help me to learn from the example of holy people and behave in a way that brings light, joy and love to others.

Help me to do good in this world, to be kind, caring and thoughtful in all I do and say.

May my life be wholly good and pleasing to you. Hear my prayers always, that they may be as sweet-smelling incense.

Amen.

'In the same way, the Spirit helps us in our weakness. We do not know what we ought to pray for, but the Spirit himself intercedes for us through wordless groans. And he who searches our hearts knows the mind of the Spirit, because the Spirit intercedes for God's people in accordance with the will of God.'

(Romans 8:26-27 NIV)

SCHOOL/COMMUNITY

Dear God,

Creator of all good things in the world and within our school community, we thank you for the gift of this day, for our families, carers, guardians and friends and for this safe place to learn and grow.

We ask you to bless all who teach and learn in our school.

We pray for our city/town/village and beyond.

Help us to be like shining jewels wherever we go, bringing joy and peace to all we meet.

Help us all to be good citizens and to put all we have learned at school to good use.

We ask this in Jesus' name.

Amen.

'And let us consider how to stir up one another to love and good works, not neglecting to meet together, as is the habit of some, but encouraging one another.'

(Hebrew 10 vs 24-25 ESV)

SELF-CONTROL

Dear God,

I ask this day for more self-control.

Lord, help me to manage my emotions and negative thoughts.

Help me to make wise decisions and not be led by the selfish things I want for myself.

Jesus, I trust in you; help me to be more like you in how I live my life.

Help me to resist both temptation and conforming to this world.

Amen.

'For God gave us a spirit not of fear but of power and love and self-control.'
(2 Timothy 1 vs 7 ESV)

SELF-DISCIPLINE

Dear God,

During this time help us to keep a positive and focused mind.

Give each one of us the strength to overcome difficulties and exercise self-discipline.

Help us to recover from hardship, pain and upset and show resilience, determination and real grit.

Help us to do what we should be doing, work as hard as we can and be the best we can be, so that we all give ourselves the best chance of a bright future.

In the meantime, remind us to praise you for every blessing.

Amen.

• • • • • • •

'We are hard pressed on every side, but not crushed; perplexed, but not in despair; persecuted, but not abandoned; struck down, but not destroyed.'

(2 Corinthians 4 vs 8-9 NIV)

SELF-ESTEEM

Dear God,

Help us to see in ourselves what you see in us.

When we lack confidence, Lord, encourage us.

When we feel low, please pick us up.

When we lack belief in our abilities and capabilities, remind us that all things are possible in you.

We thank you for friends who support us, for family who build us up and for teachers who encourage us.

Most of all, thank you for seeing the best in us and for loving us.

Amen.

'For you formed my inward parts; you knitted me together in my mother's womb. I praise you, for I am fearfully and wonderfully made. Wonderful are your works; my soul knows it very well.'

(Psalm 139 vs 13-14 ESV)

'Before I formed you in the womb I knew you, and before you were born I consecrated you; I appointed you a prophet to the nations.'

(Jeremiah 1 vs 5 ESV)

SERVICE

Father God,

Let me be of service to others today.

Let me be a help to those in need.

Help me serve you on earth, to be your hands and your feet.

Help me to be your words and your deeds to bring you glory.

Today I make myself less, so others can become more.

Today I thank you for all those who serve us. Bless them, Lord.

Amen.

'But be very careful to keep the commandment and the law that Moses the servant of the Lord gave you: to love the Lord your God, to walk in obedience to him, to keep his commands, to hold fast to him and to serve him with all your heart and with all your soul.'

(Joshua 22 vs 5 NIV)

SHARING

Father God,

Thank you for those who share; bless them richly, Lord.

Let us live following the example of Jesus who gave so freely his time, energy and love.

Help us to share what we have freely without want or expectation of anything in return.

Holy Spirit, be with us in all that we do and remind us to be generous in spirit, thoughtful and kind to all we meet.

Thank you for giving us Jesus, Father God, showing us our worth to you.

Thank you, Lord.

Amen.

'You, my brothers and sisters, were called to be free. But do not use your freedom to indulge the flesh; rather, serve one another humbly in love.'
(Galatians 5 vs 13 NIV)

SILENCE

Dear Father God,

In silence, help me to hear you.

In silence, help me to feel you.

In silence, may my prayers for others reach you.

Help me to be silent and renew focus on what's important in our busy, noisy world.

Amen.

- - -

'Even a fool who keeps silent is considered wise;
when he closes his lips, he is deemed intelligent.'

(Proverbs 17 vs 28 ESV)

'It is good that one should wait quietly for the salvation of the Lord.'

(Lamentations 3 vs 26 ESV)

SKILLS

Lord God,

What a blessing it is to possess the gift of an ability or a talent.

We thank you for those of us who have unique skills.

We pray that everyone with a talent uses it for good and to bless you.

For those of us who feel they have no talent, remind them that they have the exact skills you want for us and this is enough, Lord.

Help us to work hard at honing a current talent, a new talent or developing new skills.

Thank you that the greatest people in the Bible were those who were ready to follow your command, not those with the greatest skills.

Help us to watch, learn from and help each other, so that we might all grow in knowledge and wisdom.

Thank you, Lord, for our skills.

Amen.

• • • • • • •

'God works in different ways, but it is the same God who does the work in all of us. A spiritual gift is given to each of us so we can help each other. To one person the Spirit gives the ability to give wise advice; to another the same Spirit gives a message of special knowledge.'

(1 Corinthians 12 vs 6-8 NLT)

SPRING

Dear God,

For the most beautiful of seasons that is Spring, we thank you.

We praise you for new life, new beginnings and the explosion of life during this time.

Creator God, we praise you today for creating this spectacular season.

We thank you for the arrival of new flowers of every kind and the warming sun.

Help us this day to appreciate all of your creation and thank you quietly in our hearts.

Amen.

'He is your praise; he is your God, who performed for you those great and awesome wonders you saw with your own eyes.'
(Deuteronomy 10 vs 21 NIV)

STEWARDSHIP

Dear God,

Remind us, Lord, that we are stewards of the earth, not the owners and that everything belongs to you.

Teach us how to care for each other, the poor and those in need.

Help us to care for our local environment and world by making simple daily sacrifices like walking to school, or by using less water.

Make us grateful for all that we have, for all you have given us and for the blessings of family, friends and our school.

Help us to manage, care, protect and look after all you have given us, no matter how much or how little.

Amen.

'And God blessed them. And God said to them, "Be fruitful and multiply and fill the earth and subdue it and have dominion over the fish of the sea and over the birds of the heavens and over every living thing that moves on the earth."'

(Genesis 1 vs 28 ESV)

STILLNESS

Dear Lord,

We thank you for the peace and calm you give us as we talk to you in prayer.

Help us to always remember that you are there for us and to know that you will always give us what is right and good.

Give us the ability to use this gift as you would want us to, helping those who we meet each day, that we might be a blessing to everyone around us.

In your name, Jesus.

Amen.

'Do not be anxious about anything, but in everything by prayer and supplication with thanksgiving let your requests be known to God. And the peace of God, which surpasses all understanding, will guard your hearts and your minds in Christ Jesus.'

(Philippians 4 vs 6-7 ESV)

SUCCESS

Dear Lord,

Help us to work hard, to focus on what we need to do at school and be successful.

Thank you that we belong to a successful school, with fantastic teachers and staff. Hard work, dedication and perseverance have helped us to achieve goals and be as successful as we are.

Lord, give each one of us the strength to do the same in order to reach our full potential. Help us to support one another, spur each other on and be the best we can be at school, at home and in our communities.

Finally, God, in every task, with your help and guidance, help me do it well.

Amen.

'This Book of the Law shall not depart from your mouth, but you shall meditate on it day and night, so that you may be careful to do according to all that is written in it. For then you will make your way prosperous, and then you will have good success.'

(Joshua 1 vs 8 ESV)

SUMMER

Lord Jesus,

Thank you for summer and all the joy it can bring.

Help us to relax our bodies, restore our minds and refresh our souls.

Be with us, God, as we enjoy this beautiful season with family and friends.

Help us to show your love, goodness, hope, joy and peace with all we meet.

We pray for those who don't have holidays to look forward to, those whose lives are difficult and those who have to work.

For every blessing, every breath, every season, we thank you.

Amen.

• • • • • • •

'God writes the gospel not in the Bible alone but also in the trees and in the flowers, clouds and stars.'

(Martin Luther)

'Whatever is good and perfect is a gift coming down to us from God our Father, who created all the lights in the heavens. He never changes or casts a shifting shadow.'

(James 1 vs 17 NLT)

SUSTAINABILITY

Dear Lord,

As we think about sustainability, thank you, Father God, that you sustain all things.

Thank you for life and for the abundance of good things we have.

Make us aware of how delicate these things are, and help us to preserve, protect and promote sustainability. Living more sustainable lives ourselves, thinking about both our actions and the choices, we can make a difference to the world in which we live.

Lord, help us to look after wildlife, nature and the environment. Help us to treat people well, be less greedy and to share more.

Being sustainable is not easy with so many people sharing the earth's resources; show us how to solve these problems, which cause so much conflict and stress in many parts of the world.

In Jesus' name.

Amen.

'The Lord spoke to Moses on Mount Sinai, saying, "Speak to the people of Israel and say to them, When you come into the land that I give you, the land shall keep a Sabbath to the Lord. For six years you shall sow your field, and for six years you shall prune your vineyard and gather in its fruits, but in the seventh year there shall be a Sabbath of solemn rest for the land, a Sabbath to the Lord.'

(Leviticus 25 vs 1-4 ESV)

TALENTS

Dear God,

Thank you for giving each of us unique abilities, talents and gifts, which sets us apart from one another.

Thank you for the talent that exists in this school. Help us to celebrate that talent and praise you for each individual.

Help us to use our talents to benefit others and make this world a better place.

Amen.

'As each has received a gift, use it to serve one another, as good stewards of God's varied grace: whoever speaks, as one who speaks oracles of God; whoever serves, as one who serves by the strength that God supplies – in order that in everything God may be glorified through Jesus Christ.'

(1 Peter 4 vs 10-11 ESV)

THANKFULNESS

Feeling or expressing gratitude; appreciative.

Adjective: grateful and appreciative.

Dear God,

I decide to thank you for this day.

I am thankful for family, friends and for freedom.

I thank you for every blessing in my life.

I thank you, God, that you are in control.

I am thankful that you desire to know me and you love me.

Thank you for everything!

Amen.

'Give thanks to the LORD, for he is good; his love endures forever.'
(1 Chronicles 16 vs 34 NIV)

THANKSGIVING

Lord God,

Help us to learn from failure and not be downhearted.

When we make mistakes and things go wrong, forgive us and help us to put things right.

Help us to realise that failure is part of learning, a stepping-stone to success.

Give us the confidence to overcome failure with prayer, patience and determination.

Amen.

'My flesh and my heart may fail, but God is the strength of my heart and my portion forever.'
(Psalm 73 vs 26 NIV)

TIME

Father God,

Today, help me to use my time wisely and be thankful for it.

Help me to do all the good I can with the time I have available to me.

Thank you for the gift of time, the opportunities it brings and the memories that are created.

As I make more time for family, friends and you, direct my path and be with me.

Amen.

'Teach us to number our days, that we may gain a heart of wisdom.'
(Psalm 90 vs 12 NIV)

TOLERANCE

Dear Lord,

Help us today to show love and kindness to others.

Help us today to put others before ourselves.

Help us today to be selfless in thought, word and deed.

Help us to love our neighbour as we do ourselves.

Help us to be a light before others.

Amen.

'So whatever you wish that others would do to you,
do also to them, for this is the Law and the Prophets.'

(Matthew 7 vs 12 ESV)

TREASURE

Dear God,

Today, remind us that real treasure is self-control, goodness, gentleness, faithfulness, kindness, peace, joy and love.

We ask for more of these attributes in our lives so that our light will shine before others and others will see Jesus in us.

Come fill our hearts today, Holy Spirit.

Amen.

'For where your treasure is, there will your heart be also.'
(Luke 12 vs 34 NIV)

TRUST

Dear God,

When we find it difficult to know what to believe, help us to trust in you, and what you say in the Bible.

Help us to know you are true and you are there, God.

Come into my heart and show me your presence.

Reveal yourself today, Jesus!

Amen.

'Trust in the Lord with all your heart, and do not lean on your own understanding.'

(Proverbs 3 vs 5 ESV)

'Therefore I tell you, whatever you ask in prayer, believe that you have received it, and it will be yours.'

(Mark 11 vs 24 ESV)

TRUST

Father God,

Help me to trust in you this day.

Guide me in my journey of life.

Be with me always in good times and bad.

Be my refuge and my rock.

Answer the prayers of your people and bless us.

Be on our side and help us through every day.

In Jesus' name.

Amen.

'Trust in the LORD with all your heart, and do not lean on your own understanding. In all your ways acknowledge him, and he will make straight your paths.'

(Proverbs 3 vs 5-6 ESV)

'But I trust in your unfailing love; my heart rejoices in your salvation.'

(Psalm 13 vs 5 NIV)

UNDERSTANDING

Lord God,

Give me understanding and wisdom as I read your Word.

Help me to understand the feelings, desires and the goals of others. At the same time, help me to understand myself in my actions and reactions.

Widen my vision beyond my own small world to embrace, with knowledge and love, the lives of others.

Give me the strength to behave well, to help when I can and to play my part in this world.

Amen.

'Teach me your decrees, O Lord; I will keep them to the end. Give me understanding and I will obey your instructions; I will put them into practice with all my heart. Make me walk along the path of your commands, for that is where my happiness is found.'

(Psalm 119 vs 33-35 NLT)

UNION

Dear Lord,

Thank you that you came down to earth in human form to take away the sin of the world.

Help us to be grateful for your love and compassion for each one of us today.

Thank you that we are in union with you when we believe and trust in you with all our heart, mind and soul.

Help us to be more like you: compassionate, helpful, caring and supportive to others.

Amen.

'And we know that the Son of God has come, and has given us understanding so that we may know him who is true. And we are in him who is true by being his Son Jesus Christ. He is the true God and eternal life.'

(1 John 5 vs 20 NIV)

VALUE

Dear Lord,

Thank you that we are each valuable to you, cherished and adored.

Help us to see value not just in money and possessions, but also in deeds and kindness, love and faithfulness.

Help us to overcome greed and want. Teach us that human need, human comfort, compassion and charity are of more value.

Help us to value ourselves, to see what you see in us. We are sorry when we do wrong and make mistakes. Please guide us, Lord.

May we be a blessing to the people in our community and beyond; may we each model and live out virtuous lives which reflect true moral values to our community.

Amen.

'Finally, brothers, whatever is true, whatever is honourable, whatever is just, whatever is pure, whatever is lovely, whatever is commendable, if there is any excellence, if there is anything worthy of praise, think about these things.'

(Philippians 4 vs 8 ESV)

WINTER

Dear God,

Winter is an incredible season; we thank you for all that happens during this time.

Thank you that even in the bleakness and cold, beauty and warmth can be found.

Help us to comfort those who find winter difficult, those who work outside during these darker months and to be thankful that we have fuel and food and all that we need, unlike some on this earth.

We think particularly of the homeless and refugees – we pray for provision for them.

God, help us to appreciate this special season and make the most of the hours of daylight we have.

Amen.

'Both day and night belong to you; you made the starlight and the sun. You set the boundaries of the earth, and you made both summer and winter.'

(Psalm 74 vs 16-17 NLT)

WISDOM

Dear Lord,

It is so easy to be influenced by others, either to do good or bad things.

Give me the wisdom to be influenced by the right things and right people who have good hearts and sound judgement.

Help me also to influence others in a positive way, when they might not be doing the right thing.

God, help me manage peer pressure and always do what is right, even when it not the 'easy' thing to do. Guide me, Lord.

Help us all to learn from you, God, and use any wisdom gained from books, school and adults for good.

Help us all to behave wisely, so that we might lead honest, moral lives.

Lord, let us glorify you through our actions, thoughts and deeds today.

Finally, help us God to make wise decisions even when these decisions might be tough.

Amen.

'Give instruction to a wise man, and he will be still wiser; teach a righteous man, and he will increase in learning.'

(Proverbs 9 vs 9 ESV)

'But the wisdom from above is first pure, then peaceable, gentle, open to reason, full of mercy and good fruits, impartial and sincere.'

(James 3:17 ESV)

WONDER

Dear Lord,

You have made yourself known to us through your creation and in your Word.

Help us to see you in the beauty that exists in this world, and help us to see your hand at work in it.

As we marvel at the world's wonders, help us to remember that this was all created by you, and it is beautiful.

Today we wonder and marvel at your works – thank you, God.

Amen.

'I have made you known to them, and will continue to make you known in order that the love you have for me may be in them and that I myself may be in them.'

(John 17 vs 26 NIV)

'For the Lord himself will descend from heaven with a cry of command, with the voice of an archangel, and with the sound of the trumpet of God. And the dead in Christ will rise first. Then we who are alive, who are left, will be caught up together with them in the clouds to meet the Lord in the air, and so we will always be with the Lord. Therefore encourage one another with these words.'

(1 Thessalonians 4 vs 16-18 ESV)

WORD OF GOD

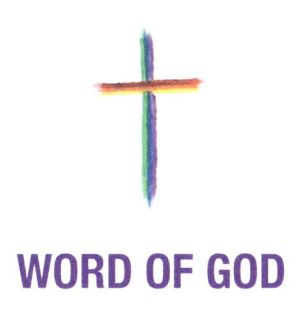

Dear Lord,

Help us to be wise and sensible and help us to use our understanding well.

Thank you for your words in the Bible which teach us how to live, and gives us wisdom.

May we be wise, and help each one of us to lead an honest, moral life, thoughtful and charitable in our words and deeds.

Remind us in our conscience when we stray from truth and doing what is right.

Lord, let us bless you in the way we live our lives. Help us to make wise decisions even when these decisions might be tough.

Amen.

'But the wisdom from above is first of all pure. It is also peace loving, gentle at all times, and willing to yield to others. It is full of mercy and the fruit of good deeds. It shows no favouritism and is always sincere.'

(James 3 vs 17 NLT)

WORLD PEACE

Dear God,

We pray for peace throughout the world, particularly in those areas of the world where there is war and suffering. We ask that world leaders would act responsibly and make wise decisions for their own people, and for the peace of the world.

We pray for refugees who have no place or country to call their own; come alongside them, Lord, and give them your peace and security. Please help them to find peace in a place that they can call home.

We pray for the lost, the oppressed, the lonely and hurting that they are not forgotten, that someone will see their need and provide support to bring them peace in our busy world.

Amen.

'Blessed are the peacemakers, for they will be called the children of God.'
(Matthew 5 vs 9 NIV)

WORLD SUFFERING

Dear God,

We pray for all those suffering from war and disasters around the world, for all those who have lost their homes and members of their family or have relatives missing.

We pray for those suffering famine and diseases as the result of war or natural disaster. We ask for strength and wisdom for those who work with them to find vital food supplies and help to restore their health.

We pray for charities who send aid and workers to areas of the world where there is real suffering. Please help those who have plenty to give generously and help the charities to use their funds wisely.

Amen.

'Each of you should give what you have decided in your heart to give, not reluctantly or under compulsion, for God loves a cheerful giver.'

(2 Corinthians 9 vs 7 NIV)

WORSHIP

Father God,

Today I worship you through my actions, my thoughts, my words and my deeds.

I look to you for my help, for guidance in my life and for comfort.

Thank you for never letting me down; thank you that I can always trust in you.

Be praised, Lord, and receive my worship and my prayers today.

In all that I do and in all that I am, let me worship you and bring you glory.

Amen.

'But be sure to fear the LORD and serve him faithfully with all your heart; consider what great things he has done for you.'

(1 Samuel 12 vs 24 NIV)

"AMEN"

If you want to make a prayer your own and affirm what has been said, you say 'Amen'.

'Amen' means: I / We agree.

'Amen' is an integral part of prayer and usually comes at the end.